STATIONS OF THE COSMIC CHRIST

PRAISE FOR *STATIONS OF THE COSMIC CHRIST*

"What a brilliant and exciting combination of creative words and evocative images. And where they take us is where we must go! We need a Christ at least as large as the universe we inhabit and much larger than the tribal religion most of us were born into. Allow yourself to be happily led there."
— Richard Rohr, O.F.M., Center for Action and Contemplation, Albuquerque, New Mexico

"*Stations of the Cosmic Christ* is a wonderful book. It's a journey to a profound awareness of what Christ, and what love, really mean."
— Marianne Williamson, *New York Times* best-selling author, *Return to Love* and *A Year of Miracles*

"Matthew Fox is the greatest living Christian Mystic Theologian and this book a feast of visionary wisdom. Read it and cherish it and give it to all your friends."
— Andrew Harvey, author of *The Hope: A Guide to Sacred Activism*

"*Stations of the Cosmic Christ* is a divinely inspired book that must be read by every human being devoted to spiritual and global survival. It is cosmically brilliant."
— Caroline Myss, author of *Anatomy of the Spirit* and *Defy Gravity*

"This visionary book sheds startling new light on the possibility of mystic awakening for Christians—as well as other seekers—eager to discover and practice a faith for the 21st century. Matthew Fox may be our greatest living spiritual reformer. Brave, brilliant, and truly unique."
— Mark Matousek, author of *Ethical Wisdom: The Search for a Moral Life*

'Matthew Fox inspires us again with this gorgeous and grace-filled celebration with Bishop Marc Andrus. *Stations of the Cosmic Christ* is a compelling call to reimagined consciousness and a guide to attaining it, combining evocative images with hallmark eloquence that guides us toward the transformation necessary for our individual and collective well-being and survival. Full of wisdom and practical insight, this book is simply essential for anyone committed to spiritual practice, to healing and justice, and to the continued preservation of the Earth and the uplifting of all people held by it."
— Dora E. McQuaid, author of *The Scorched Earth*

"In this creative work, the authors offer concrete entry points into a set of reflective spiritual practices for those called to move into an expansive understanding of the person of Jesus Christ today. Through imaginative encounters that go beyond a traditional focus on Christ's passion and death, and which honor the radical freedom offered by his life and teaching, the Stations in this book provide a rich space for meditation. The beauty and strength of the art that focuses the practices presented here, the generous interfaith sensibilities of the authors, and the ways that they weave together the scriptural accounts of Jesus, the great liturgical actions and feasts, and the concerns of contemporary people, make this book a precious gift to those seeking to cultivate a cosmic sense of the living presence of Christ."
— Susanna Singer, Ph.D., spiritual director and professor at the Church Divinity School of the Pacific, Berkeley, California

STATIONS OF THE COSMIC CHRIST

Matthew Fox and Bishop Marc Andrus

with artists Ullrrich Javier Lemus and M.C. Richards

UNITY® Books

ISBN-13 (trade softcover): 978-0-87-159380-1

Edited by Nora Boxer; paperback revisions by Ellen Debenport

Sculptures: M.C. Richards and Ullrrich Javier Garcia Lemus

Hardback Cover Design by Wabi Sabi Design Studio; paperback revisions by Kyle Stephan

OTHER BOOKS BY MATTHEW FOX

Original Blessing

The Coming of the Cosmic Christ

A Spirituality Named Compassion

Prayer: A Radical Response to Life

Creation Spirituality: Liberating Gifts for the Peoples of the Earth

Whee! We, Wee All the Way Home: Toward a Prophetic, Sensual Spirituality

Western Spirituality: Historical Roots, Ecumenical Routes (edited)

Natural Grace (with Rupert Sheldrake)

The Physics of Angels (with Rupert Sheldrake)

Christian Mystics: 365 Readings and Meditations

Passion for Creation: Meister Eckhart's Earth-Based Spirituality

Meister Eckhart: A Mystic-Warrior for Our Times

Meditations with Meister Eckhart

Illuminations of Hildegard of Bingen

Hildegard of Bingen, A Saint for Our Times: Unleashing Her Power in the 21st Century

Hildegard of Bingen's Book of Divine Works, Songs and Letters

Sheer Joy: Conversations with Thomas Aquinas on Creation Spirituality

A Way to God: Thomas Merton's Creation Spirituality Journey

The Reinvention of Work: A New Vision of Livelihood for Our Times

Creativity: Where the Divine and the Human Meet

The Hidden Spirituality of Men: Ten Metaphors to Awaken the Sacred Masculine

The A.W.E. Project: Reinventing Education, Reinventing the Human

Occupy Spirituality: A Radical Vision for a New Generation (with Adam Bucko)

Sins of the Spirit, Blessings of the Flesh: Transforming Evil in Soul and Society

Wrestling With the Prophets: Essays on Creations Spirituality and Everyday Life

The Pope's War: Why Ratzinger's Secret Crusade Has Imperiled the Church and What Can Be Saved

Confessions: The Making of a Post-Denominational Priest

One River, Many Wells: Wisdom Springing From Global Faiths

Religion USA: Culture and Religion by Way of <u>Time</u> Magazine

A New Reformation

Letters to Pope Francis

Creation Spirituality: A New Story, a Deep Lineage

Naming the Unnameable: 89 Wonderful and Useful Names for God … Including the Unnameable God

The Lotus & the Rose: Dialogs on Buddhism and Christian Mysticism (with Lama Tsomo)

DEDICATION

We dedicate this book to M.C. Richards on the occasion of the centenary of her birth and in gratitude not only for her "I Am" tablets displayed in this book and at Grace Cathedral but for her life and work that inspires so many. Her wise teaching that "love is fostered by a capacity to experience cosmos" seems especially apt for the theme of this book.

We also dedicate it to the young who are moving into a whole new spiritual arena as they respond to the call of Mother Earth for a deeper wisdom and practice and an expanded generosity. May they always feel the support of the elders!

TABLE OF CONTENTS

PART TWO

STATIONS OF THE COSMIC CHRIST

MATTHEW FOX
BISHOP MARC ANDRUS

WITH ARTISTS M.C. RICHARDS & ULLRRICH JAVIER LEMUS

INTRODUCTION

BISHOP MARC ANDRUS

SPIRITUAL PRACTICES AND NON-RELIGIOUS PEOPLE

Spiritual practice is a fecund space between committed religious life and life lived on the surface. To be in the space of spiritual practice doesn't mean that one will ever end up an adherent of one of the great world religions, but it might mean that the virtues of the Cosmic Christ and of mystic experience may bloom in one's life.

The office where I work on many weekdays looks out on one of the two labyrinths at Grace Cathedral in San Francisco (the other labyrinth is just inside the great Ghiberti Doors). Some days I need to arrive at the cathedral quite early, while the world is still waking up and lightening. Amazingly, people are often walking the labyrinth even at this early hour. And near those using the outdoor labyrinth are a great number of people, mostly Chinese, who are practicing Tai Chi and Qi Gong.

Some of my workdays stretch late into the evening, and again, at the close of the day I can make out people walking, dancing, and kneeling in prayer in the labyrinth. The contemporary labyrinth movement was born at Grace Cathedral under the guidance of the Reverend Lauren Artress. Since the movement's inception in the early 1990s it is estimated that there are nearly 5,000 new labyrinths around the world. Just in San Francisco alone, I know of two others besides the labyrinths at Grace Cathedral, one at Land's End (a dramatic hiking trail at the top of the San Francisco peninsula), and another on the campus of a city hospital. The thousands of people who use these San Francisco labyrinths each year are not necessarily religious people—our region is considered the most secular part of the United States—but they are surely engaging in a spiritual practice.

Other spiritual practices can be seen at Grace Cathedral that are not tied to formal religious services. All day long people come into the cathedral and find one of our icons—of the Virgin and Child; of Mary Magdalene; of Martin Luther King Jr.; or of the Cosmic Christ (most often labeled the *Pantokrator*, Judge of the Cosmos), among others. I see these people kneeling or standing quietly before these images, lighting candles, staying silent for some period of time, and then leaving the cathedral.

A fantastic spiritual practice has sprung up at Grace Cathedral over the last five years: Yoga on the Labyrinth. Grace Cathedral sits on the top of one of San Francisco's steepest hills—hills that leave our tourists puffing and sweating. Yet each Tuesday afternoon some 700 people, mostly young adults, make their way with their yoga mats to practice yoga at Grace Cathedral.

The phenomenon of Yoga on the Labyrinth illustrates a fruitful relationship between religion and spiritual practice. The staff of Grace Cathedral seek to honor the Yoga on the Labyrinth participants as people on a valid spiritual path; we do not seek to convert them to Christianity or the Episcopal Church. We do, however, work closely with the wonderful yogi Darren Main, who teaches Yoga on the Labyrinth, to see how we can support and deepen the spiritual practice of those who attend week to week.

We have found several creative ways to support the spiritual lives and quests of the Yoga on the Labyrinth participants. First, a priest from the cathedral opens each evening practice with a short meditation. The meditation is tied to an overall theme for each week's practice. For instance, on the Tuesday after the Fourth of July in 2015, the Reverend Jude Harmon gave the opening meditation. His theme was freedom. He spoke of the Declaration of Independence and said it was a marker on the way to freedom, as was the later Emancipation Proclamation. He ended by naming the ongoing work of gaining freedom for all. Darren then began the actual yoga practice by inviting everyone into Child's Pose (a kneeling pose where the forehead touches the ground), but in a variation where the palms of the hands faced upward—so that, he said, we could offer up all that was not free within us. During the practice, musicians played on tuned glass bowls and other instruments, while a man and woman chanted, mostly in Sanskrit. Near the end of the practice, the chanting moved into the hymn "Amazing Grace"—a hymn that sings of liberation from bondage. Finally, Darren read a passage on freedom from the writings of the Dalai Lama. Those of us practicing that evening experienced a sustained, profound exploration of the idea of freedom—much more so than if we had done a simple run-through of yoga asanas.

Another very important way that we at Grace Cathedral help support the Yoga on the Labyrinth practitioners is through offering opportunities for giving and for service—spiritual practices in themselves that are taught by all the great religions of the world. We believe that a human life that is open-handed toward the world is a happier, better life than a closed-handed life, so we seek to provide ways that these practitioners can serve the wider community.

The practices of the Stations of the Cosmic Christ—walking the Stations or using them in card form—are offerings from the two of us, people who have been nurtured by the Christian tradition, to deepen your own spiritual life and to guide you in the direction that your spirit and your imagination point out to you. May the Stations of the Cosmic Christ and your practice with them be blessings to you, increasing the light in your life, helping you find meaning in suffering, strengthening you to work for justice for all and for the Earth.

MATTHEW FOX
WHY THE STATIONS OF THE COSMIC CHRIST?

This is a book of meditations on the Cosmic Christ. These meditations accompany the wonderful clay tablets or plaques that were first displayed in San Francisco's Grace Cathedral, a place of historic influence in the very special City on the Bay, where the celebrated Labyrinth Ritual has emanated forth to affect hundreds of thousands of practitioners around the world. We include those tablets of the Cosmic Christ in this book, and we hope they inspire many other artists to step up and create their own inspired version of the Stations of the Cosmic Christ around the world and in many houses of worship—be they presented in clay, painting, or wood.

Beyond that, we also include in our work cards of the Cosmic Christ so that personal practices may take place at home or on the road, whether alone or with others, beyond the confines of ecclesial buildings.

We are hopeful that the naming of the Stations of the Cosmic Christ as presented by the artists of these tablets, as well as our meditations on the stations, might affect a spirit awakening and an evolving of the Christ Consciousness (and Buddha consciousness and consciousness of the image of God in all beings) that is so needed in our fractious and bleeding times. Our species seems in so many respects to be losing its way, and religion—along with education, politics, finance, and beyond—needs a stark awakening. The earth is losing so much beauty and health and diversity at the hands of humans who seem hell-bent on our own destruction: we poison our seas and lands, our forests and farms, our minds and hearts, and contribute to an irrevocable climate change that dooms many. We hope these practices and those they awaken in others' imaginations might contribute to the healing and the waking up that is so necessary.

BALANCING THE TRADITIONAL "STATIONS OF THE CROSS"

Western Christianity has been practicing for centuries the devotion of the Stations of the Cross, which can be found in just about any Roman Catholic or Anglican Church in existence. The Stations of the Cross present a spiritual practice that invites one into the last hours of Jesus' life, beginning with his trial before Pontius Pilate and ending with his crucifixion and burial. It is a powerful practice to enter into and thereby relive the final 20 hours of Jesus' life on Earth. There have also been contemporary adaptations of this practice: for example, among the suffering peasants of Latin America struggling for their rights, or applied to the demise of the Earth who today is struggling for her survival.

But the practice of the Stations of the Cross by no means presents a full or accurate remembrance of the richness of the Christ story and the Jesus experience and teachings. It covers 20 hours of a life of 30 (or so) years and a public life of about three years, and its emphasis on the cross alone is suspect, since the cross was not a significant symbol in Christianity until the fourth century (and the crucifix until the 10th century). The practice of the Stations of the Cross leaves out so much of the teachings of Jesus, of the release of Christ energy that he accomplished, and even of the richer meaning of the crucifixion. It fails therefore to address the very question of why he was put to death. Other pivotal events in the life of Jesus and the response and happenings of his earliest followers, including those who put the Gospels together and wrote the public letters that constitute so much of Christian Scriptures, are completely missing from the practice of the Stations of the Cross.

Among these events are the Nativity Stories, the Baptism of Jesus, the Transfiguration, the Crucifixion as a cosmic event, the Resurrection and Ascension and Pentecost experience. These rich and meaningful moments—indeed archetypal events—in the Jesus story deserve our attention and devotion and practice as well or more than just the walk of carrying his cross. These are moments of breakthrough of the Cosmic Christ. The Cosmic Christ teachings represent the earliest hymns of the followers of Jesus and the most universal stories and teachings, including, for example, the "I Am" sayings of John's Gospel and the teaching of Matthew 25, "Do it to the least and you do it to me," which is an archetypal declaration of the meaning of compassion and which is a parable composed and shared by the historical Jesus.

This book brings a balance to Christian practice by including some of the richest of the teachings and breakthroughs of Jesus and his immediate followers in the early Christ community, and by embedding them into contemporary practice and culture.

Our meditations are meant to be suggestive: to awaken your own thoughts and prayers and questions and imaginations into journeying into a deeper relationship with the Cosmic Christ and the teachings of the earliest Christians. We are not intending to offer a last word—only some pictures and first words—to trigger, awaken, ignite, and excite your own connections, your own resolutions, your own coming alive, and your own meditation and prayer and action that derives from such. The reader will find that our meditations are presented alternatively, that is to say, Matthew leads off with one Station and Bishop Marc leads off with the next one and so it goes back and forth.

This is an interactive book, therefore—a workbook or a prayer book—not only by us and for you but by you and for you as well. It is a cocreation—not only by two authors from different backgrounds with different vocations—but with the artists whose work is included. We hope it will inspire many other artists as well. It is also a cocreation on your part. We, the dual authors, wish to cocreate with you as you continue your spiritual journey of evolving into a fuller and truer and ever more unique expression of the Cosmic Christ. The book, after all, is a book of practices, and practices are important for a deeper spiritual life. In the first part of the book, the focus is on the practice of the Stations of the Cosmic Christ; the second part of the book offers additional practices for nourishing the journey.

You can pray this book alone or with others or you can pray it in the card form which we are also making available. In this way the practice we are proposing becomes very portable—you do not have to visit a church to engage with it. You can pray this book at church or at home—or on the bus or on a plane or on the highway.

We have divided the book into two parts. The first part, with the work of two major artists, addresses the traditional seven "I Ams" intermingled with nine "Major Cosmic Christ Events." We limit the overall Stations to 16.

The "I Am" is the divine name: Moses asked God for a name and the reply was, "I am who I am" (or "I am who I will be") (Exodus 3:14). Thus, when we see an "I Am," we are dealing with a Divine Name meant to apply to each of us, since we are all "other Christs" or "sons and daughters of God" or "sacred beings" or "rays of God" (Hildegard) or "images of God" or "other Buddhas." We present additional "I Am" sayings, as well as a mandala practice, mantra chants, and further practices in Part Two.

The traditional Stations of the Cross number 14 stations, but by themselves the Stations of the Cross can present a one-sided, death-and-guilt orientation to the Jesus story. After all, it is not simply due to the last 20 hours of his life that Jesus is relevant today. Jesus is also extremely important today for his teachings of courage and compassion, of expansion and of trust, of the nobility of every person and every creature, and of the sacredness of all beings. He is important because he stood up to the Roman Empire of his day (as did his mentor, John the Baptist, who also paid the ultimate price for doing so) and offered an alternative set of values. These are found in the basic teachings of the Cosmic Christ, whether presented as "I Am" sayings or as significant—indeed archetypal—events in the stories that surround Jesus: the stories of his nativity, transfiguration, baptism, resurrection, and more.

Rabbi David Seidenberg, a Jewish scholar, has recently published a breakthrough book titled *Kabbalah and Ecology: God's Image in the More-Than-Human World*. The central question of the book is this: Is God's image to be found in all beings, according to Jewish teachings? Exploring the Bible and the midrash, the Kabbalah and the rich history of Jewish intellectual thought, Rabbi Seidenberg concludes that this indeed is the case. He feels, as we do, that this awareness offers the proper substrate for an ecological theology in an ecological time. In our language and the language of this book, he is speaking of the "Cosmic Christ," for the Cosmic Christ bespeaks the image of God, the light of Divinity and spark of Divinity in every being in the universe.

The need to grow our awareness of the holiness of all beings is why we feel that the teaching and the praying that accompanies these pages is so important. We need to begin to ingest the Cosmic Christ teachings deep within our souls and consciousness if we are to recover a deep sense of the sacredness of all existence and of the unique sacredness of our time on Earth and of the Earth herself. Time is running out for our species. Religion needs to wake up and to assist all of us to wake up. We hope this book and the practices it launches serve that process.

MATTHEW FOX AND BISHOP MARC ANDRUS

The Cosmic Christ and Liturgical Feast Days

A deep part of any spiritual tradition is the great feast days of the liturgical year. If one looks with the lens of the Cosmic Christ at the great feast days of the Christian tradition, one sees time and time again that they are built around the Cosmic Christ Events that are named in these Stations. Biblical scholars tell us that the events celebrated on those days are more mythical than historical, and that is just fine—they are even archetypal, thus transcending any particular time and culture. It is the great stories and the moving myths, after all, that excite the imagination and trigger holy curiosity and wonder. The late psychologist Rollo May wrote about how values are taught through myths much more than any other way,[1] and Burton Mack, a scholar of the early church community, tells us that what transpired after Jesus' death was "an explosion of creative imagination that we would call myth-making."[2]

Consider how many of the Cosmic Christ Events depicted in clay (and shown in this book and on the walls of our churches where the "Stations of the Cosmic Christ" will hang) invariably have an important feast day attached to them. The Nativity, the Baptism of Jesus, the Transfiguration (the biggest day of the year in Eastern Orthodox Christianity), Crucifixion, Resurrection, Ascension, and Pentecost are all examples of this connection. Though rooted in history, their universal archetypal appeal is that they speak to profound yearnings of the human heart, wherever humans reflect on life and death and meaning and justice and surprise and awe and gratitude.

Indeed, a strong argument could be made that the Eucharist itself, the ancient practice of remembering Jesus through the bread and wine that many Christians celebrate on a weekly basis, is also an "I Am" moment. In saying "this is my body" over the bread and "this chalice is my blood" over the wine, Jesus is uttering "I Am": "I am this bread; I am this wine." And so are we, partakers as we are of the sacred bread and wine of the universe.

The Sacred Cosmos and Teachings From Science

Einstein said that we need a cosmic religion. He declared that humanity was:

... now moving into the third phase of religious experience: cosmic religion. With his growing knowledge of the vastness of the universe and its trillions of stars, each one many times larger than our planet, stars whose light takes hundreds of years to reach our eyes, man must consider it an insult when he is told that his conduct should be motivated by fear of punishment or hope of reward. And it is just as much an insult to the God who created all these marvels, to be lowered to a human level. The true religious genius has always been endowed with this sense of cosmic religion ... This oneness of creation, to my sense, is God. This concept of God will unite all nations ... A new age of peace will be inaugurated when all people profess a cosmic religion, when the youth have become laymen with scientific minds.[3]

To resuscitate Christianity by way of the devotional practices of the Cosmic Christ means, among other things, that we reawaken to the cosmos itself. This should not be so difficult today because science is gifting us with so many breakthrough understandings of the universe, thanks to telescopes operating from space and also from more and more technologically advanced telescopes on Earth. Anyone at all curious about our cosmos has ample information and amazing images to imbibe in our time—one can simply go to Google or YouTube to find them. A renewed interest in the Cosmic Christ can assist a deeper appreciation of the sacredness of the entire cosmos, and vice versa.

The cosmos itself becomes a Sacrament, the original "manger" wherein the Cosmic Christ is born, nurtured, and comes to fruition. Each of us and each being we encounter, whether in our home, the Earth, or millions of light years away in space is born in this "manger," this matrix of hundreds of billions of galaxies that has been expanding and creating for 13.8 billion years. Science and spirituality are not at odds; quite the opposite, they need each other. Science provides facts and spirituality provides meaning. Actually, science today provides strange and stirring parables and images that function as pointers to meaning, much as myth has done for millennia. Therefore, today both science and spirituality point us toward meaning. It is at the level of meaning that people need to listen to the new scientific discoveries and consider what the implications are for a renewal of awe, wonder, appreciation, creativity, celebration, and compassion.

The cosmos is about the macrocosm, the largest beings we know of such as galaxies and clusters of galaxies; and it is also about the microcosm, the smallest beings we know of. The same is true of the Cosmic Christ. The Cosmic Christ speaks to the macrocosm: The universe as a whole is sacred and sacramental and singular, and it can be called the "mystical body of Christ" or "the pattern that connects." But the Cosmic Christ is the microcosmic world as well: Every atom contains photons or light waves and is "another Christ" who is the light in every being. All being is holy. A Cosmic Christ consciousness then brings us back to a sense of reverence—for ourselves, for all Earth creatures, for all beyond-Earth beings, and for existence itself. The Cosmic Christ has the potential to usher in a new era of reverence and respect for the world and its creatures. At a time like ours when so much life and diversity is threatened on our planet, what is more important than this? Reverence can be regained and once again enter all of our equations, whether they be about economics, politics, religion, media, art, or education.

One way to understand the Cosmic Christ is to see it as an invitation to our better—indeed our best—selves. (This parallels Buddhism, which sees Buddha nature within all of us, and the Jewish tradition, which sees the image of God in all beings.) We are on a journey to discover and give birth to the Christ in ourselves—the most loving, joyful, justice-committed, courageous, generous, caring, and compassionate parts of ourselves. That is why the kind of practices we present here are so important. They are about renewing religion and spirituality from the inside out; from the individual back into new expressions of community and into our worlds of work, politics, education, economics, and the rest of society. Christ is in all of us: That is what the Cosmic Christ teaching is telling us. Christ is the best in all of us. The Buddha in us. The God self in us. The image of God in us. That which we emulate and desire to imitate. It is our imitation of God, imitation of Christ, 21st-century style.

How important is a recovery of the Cosmic Christ? Jesuit priest, scientist, and mystic Pierre Teilhard de Chardin (1881–1955) put it this way: "Because it is not exalted by a sufficiently passionate admiration of the universe, our religion is becoming enfeebled."[4] Thus he ascribed the demise of religion to the loss of a cosmic awareness. He also observed that getting believers to think of the Cosmic Christ was very difficult. "This third nature of Christ (neither human nor divine, but cosmic)—has not noticeably attracted the explicit attention of the faithful or of theologians." Believers seem stuck on an anthropocentric deity and in centuries-old wranglings about the nature of Jesus (was he human, or divine, or both?)—and yet they ignore the ancient teaching, found in the earliest writings and hymns of the community, about the Cosmic Christ. Teilhard goes further when he writes, "The cosmos is fundamentally and primarily living ... Christ, through the Incarnation, is internal to the world ... rooted in the world, even in the very heart of the tiniest atom ... Nothing seems to me more vital, from the point of view of human energy, than the appearance and eventually, the systematic cultivation of such a 'cosmic sense.'"[5]

Many people have responded to my book *The Coming of the Cosmic Christ*, telling me their lives were changed by it, and that it certainly changed their relationship to the Christian tradition. The venerable Father Bede Griffiths, a Benedictine monk who lived over 50 years in an ashram in India, said in a public dialog with me that "creation spirituality is the spirituality of the future, and Fox's theology of the Cosmic Christ is the theology of the future." It would seem that the devotion we are sharing here around the Stations of the Cosmic Christ has legs to it.

CULTIVATING THE COSMIC SENSE

The Stations of the Cosmic Christ we present in this book can surely contribute to the systematic cultivation of this cosmic sense, and with it, a sense of the sacred to be found in the entire universe. To recover the Cosmic Christ is to recover our sense of the sacred in all of nature—including human nature. In doing so, we deepen our commitment to the following:

1. Deep ecumenism or interfaith and interspirituality, for the Cosmic Christ takes us to the heart of all religious experience—the living encounter with the Divine in all things.
2. Ecological justice, for the Cosmic Christ reminds us that a healthy planet is a gift to all humanity and all other beings—yet it is a gift that requires attention and care, defending, and wise stewardship.
3. Ending militarism and the misuse of human imagination to build ever more demonic

weapons; there is no need to spend our limited brainpower and treasure on killing enemies rather than loving our children.

4. Ending the most advanced form of gluttony ever devised on our planet—our advertising-fed addiction to consumerism that in turn feeds an economic system that makes idols of objects. It does so at the expense of the development of intersubjective relationships that matter, such as celebrating, ritual-making, healing, and learning what true living is about.

5. Taming the reptilian brain. This 420-million-year-old part of all of us is about action/ reaction and being Number One. It can easily dominate the mammal brain, which is about family, kinship, and compassion and is only half as old as the reptilian brain. Mysticism can calm the reptilian brain, because it teaches us the value of solitude—and reptiles are quite prone to aloneness and solitude.

To bring the Cosmic Christ tradition alive is to bring the great stories and teachings and presence of Jesus and the Christ into our midst and into our times, and into a global culture alongside (not in opposition to) the wisdom and genius of many other religious and spiritual traditions. A Cosmic Christ revival can help to resurrect humankind as well as our various religions. Its effects will be felt far beyond church doors or ecclesial mindsets. It is about bringing a rebirth of wisdom: Cosmic Wisdom.

Keys to recovering the Cosmic Christ from the Scriptures were laid out in my book *The Coming of the Cosmic Christ* 28 years ago. Among them are the following:

1. Angels: Angels are cosmic beings, beings of light that travel at the speed of light. When they are present, the Cosmic Christ is being alluded to.

2. "Lord": The word *kyrios* or "Lord" means "Ruler of the Universe," "one who makes the universe go around." It is a cosmic title.

3. Cloud: In apocalyptic literature, Divinity often rides the clouds, which are frequently settings for theophanies and encounters with the Divine. In a desert culture, a cloud is a sort of miracle,

bringing not only grace-like shade but maybe even the gift of water. According to one biblical scholar, "In the later Jewish writings, the cloud was par excellence the vehicle of God's *Shekinah* (the dwelling presence of God) and the medium in and through which he manifested himself."[6]

4. Glory: The word "glory" (*doxa*) connotes the divine radiance and beauty that fills the universe. It is a cosmological term.

5. Wilderness and mountains: Divine theophanies often take place at the places of power and energy denoted by mountains, and also in the wilderness where the terror and beauty of the Divine is manifest and felt. Thus the prophet says: "I will call you out to the wilderness and there speak to you heart to heart" (Hosea 2:14).

6. Evil: The struggle with evil is a wrestling with cosmological forces, "powers and principalities" that are bigger than humans alone (Ephesians 6:12).[7]

If we are going to talk of the Cosmic Christ again, we must begin by talking about the cosmos. Thanks to scientific discoveries of the past 100 years in particular, many of which were launched by the seminal breakthroughs in thought and imagination by Albert Einstein and Ernest Hubble, we now know that we belong to a universe that is vast and in motion and expanding and full of creativity (a star is being born every 15 seconds!) and deeply mysterious (96 percent of matter is either dark energy or dark matter and thus very difficult to see and full of mystery). We know the universe we dwell in, our home, our matrix, is 13.8 billion years old, and all its "stuff" is related, since it began smaller than a pinpoint and has developed, evolved, expanded, and grown ever since.

Consider this about the vastness of our universe. Given the facts that there are 7 billion humans on Earth and at least 200 billion galaxies in our universe (each with hundreds of millions of stars), you and I and every human being on the planet could "adopt" or hold in our hearts and minds our own "nest" or "family" of galaxies. This would come to over 285 galaxies per person on the planet! This is how large our home is and also how large our imaginations are, that we can even think of such a family of relationships. Each of us is a godmother or godfather to 285 different galaxies. One would think we would be busy enough simply getting to know them and what is in them to take our minds off of spending money to go to war with our neighbors on this planet.

MATTHEW FOX AND BISHOP MARC ANDRUS

This allegory, taken from the facts of the cosmos as we understand it today, demonstrates how abundant and generous the universe is—and how amazing we humans are to be able to begin to grasp the reality we live in. We, too, are vast—otherwise we could not begin to feel the vastness of our home. Our home can be viewed as very impersonal: Getting to know 285 galaxies per person is a big task to undertake. But it is also very personal since all galaxies and stars and persons and planets and beings are made up of the same "stuff" and derive from the same 13.8-billion-year journey of atoms and galaxies and supernovas and stars and planets. These beings are all our ancestors. They helped make us; our bodies derive from their creative processes that cooked and exploded via supernovas the elements we comprise. Without them we do not exist. Yes, they are our grandparents on a cosmic scale.

The archetype of the Cosmic Christ helps to name both the vastness of our ancestral tree but also its personal side. Our relationship to the universe holds both ends of the macrocosmic/microcosmic spectrum. The Cosmic Christ, "the pattern that connects all things in the heavens and on earth" (as the Scriptures say), personalized what would otherwise be a very impersonal universe, one with dark holes and vast spaces and expanding times and space fields to traverse in eerie silence and cold, cosmic loneliness. Instead, we are reminded of a universe which cares, which blesses and upholds and uplifts us. We are invited to do the same for others and for future generations.

Maybe in the future, instead of using our imaginations to plan and make war, we humans will put our minds and creativity to work naming all the galaxies who in so many ways are our ancestors and companions and siblings on this journey. More than 285 galaxies for each human being to steward and attend to ought to keep us occupied and out of trouble, and might tame our reptilian brains—finally.

Immensity, Intensity, and Intimacy: Marks of a Mystical Experience

To think cosmically again is to become aware of:

Immensity. The cosmos billions of galaxies large, each with billions of stars.

It is also to attend to:

Intensity. Awe and wonder and truth and beauty strike us so deeply that they are unforgettable.

It is also to consider:

Intimacy. There is a deeply personal side to the vast and sometimes very impersonal universe.

Immensity, Intensity, and Intimacy are inherent to any mystical experience. In recovering the awe, wonder, and sacredness of the universe again, we are reconnecting to the mysticism of our ancestors, as well as our own capacity for mysticism. Together these Three "I's" add up to a mystical experience.[8] The Universe is one vast, deep, dark, expanding, quiet, noiseless, wondersome, mystical "one-ing" experience. We all come from the same source. The universe is also birthing. It is nothing if not a "maternity bed," to use Meister Eckhart's language. "What does God do all day long? God lies on a maternity bed giving birth."

All these qualities can be found in the archetype of the Cosmic Christ, which personalizes the universe and names what a mystical experience is all about. From a perspective of a Cosmic Christ theology, the universe becomes a manger (on a cosmic scale) where the Christ is born every day in diverse forms. The Christ is the son or daughter of God, the Buddha Nature, the light incarnate, the light of the world, the light within all things, the wisdom and *doxa* or glory in all things, the divine image in all things. To see the "light in all things" is therefore to see the Christ in all things (or the Buddha nature, or the *shekinah*). Today's science assures us that there are photons or light waves in every atom in the universe. Voilà! The Cosmic Christ.

The Cosmic Christ is as immense as the universe. The Hindu tradition talks about the "Cosmic Man," and the early Christian writings talk about the "mystical body of Christ." The Cosmic Christ is as intense as the depths of the spiritual experiences we undergo in nature, poetry, music, dance, worship, lovemaking, family, parenting, work, the struggle for justice, and more. The Cosmic Christ is intimate. It renders the whole universe accessible and intimate, for it personalizes it. It is "the pattern that connects." It is everywhere binding all things together. It is Love. That is the teaching of the Cosmic Christ: that love binds all things together. It is a force, just as gravity (which is essentially attraction) and electromagnetic energy (which we might call the spark between all beings) also are.

What is more intimate than eating food, growing food, preparing it, and transforming it into energy for our own life every day? It is important to remember that all food is cosmic food—that we eat the sun daily when we eat oatmeal or rice, tomatoes or broccoli, and when we drink orange juice or tea. All of our food is cosmic food, and it is both distant and near—indeed, intimate—for it enters us. Eating marries the outside to the inside.

Thus, too, the practice of sharing the Eucharist—"Do this in memory of me"—is a practice of eating and drinking the divine food that is the universe. When we eat this bread and drink this life force we ingest and render intimate the Cosmic Christ in all beings, the food of the universe itself. We connect to the most distant stars and galaxies of the universe when we take our food and nourishment. What is more satisfying than that? What is more intimate than that? What is more erotic than that food? What brings macro and micro into union and communion more than that? What marries psyche and cosmos more than that?

The Eucharist becomes an act of ingesting the most distant atoms of the universe and sacralizing them, reminding us of how sacred this home is in which we dwell. It breaks through limits of time and space, self and others, God and us. It is holy food indeed. As Julian of Norwich put it, "Between God and our soul there is no between." The Cosmic Christ makes it so. In the Eucharist we Cosmic Christs are united with all the Cosmic Christs of the world.

Also at stake in this Holy Communion and cosmic Sacrament is shared suffering. The Cosmic Christ is not just about the light in all things but also the wounds in all things. All beings suffer. The death and crucifixion of Jesus is archetypal to all beings in the universe. The Christ we eat is a crucified Christ, a Christ of passion and compassion, of hurt and suffering and loss. That, too, is integral to the universe we know: suffering, brokenness, death (and rebirth) are everywhere. Evolution pays testimony to that reality also as it carries the record not only of the death of individuals but of entire species. Evolution teaches us about the coming and going, the life, death, and resurrection of all forms in the universe. The Christ we eat is not pure light but broken light. The wounds of the universe are also rendered intimate when we eat the body and drink the cup—and we are strengthened to work works of compassion and justice to heal, to prevent as much suffering as possible, to replace injustice with justice, to be one-in-suffering as well as one-in-light. We are nourished, one and all, to be the strong spiritual warriors or prophets that true spirituality requires of us, to do battle with the "beasts in our past and the hooves of the night that want to break the jeweled vision in our hearts" (Hafiz).

The Christ is a "stern warrior," according to the Book of Wisdom teaching that is read at Christmas Eve liturgy, who "leapt from the heavenly throne into a doomed land." There is work to do. The Earth as we know it is suffering deep wounds; multiple species are in jeopardy; climate change is happening; and, of course, wars and poverty and prejudice and hate abound among foolish humans everywhere. Communion is not just a place of repose, but a place of action born of repose. We call that work compassion, as in Jesus' admonition: "Be you compassionate as your Creator in heaven is compassionate" (Luke 6:36). The Cosmic Christ is about healing and compassion. And "compassion means justice," as Meister Eckhart insists; indeed, "compassion is where peace and justice meet."[9]

How are we doing? How is the Cosmic Christ doing?

Deep Ecumenism, Interfaith, and Encountering the Cosmic Christ

Some people say that the term "Cosmic Christ" excludes persons who do not identify as Christian. But that is not my experience. A number of years ago a man came to visit me in Oakland, California, and he told me this story. He was not a Christian and not particularly religious, but one day as he was walking in the woods, Christ appeared to him and they had a considerable conversation. Afterwards, he went into a bookstore to find a book on Christ and he picked up my book *The Coming of the Cosmic Christ*; he said that book made sense of his encounter that day. He said of all the world's religions, the Native American tradition held the greatest appeal to him. He then presented me with a gift: a hand-carved, three-foot-high "totem pole" of the Cosmic Christ that honors the four directions, the plant people, and the four-legged people, and that had a symbol of the risen Christ at the top. I reproduce the carving here on page 198. For me it carries many worthwhile stories, stories I have heard from many persons who have also encountered the Christ outside of a Christian context.

One does not have to be a Christian to experience the Cosmic Christ (or a Buddhist to experience the Buddha nature). Recently, I lectured in South Korea, and the day after my lecture, a Buddhist monk who had attended said to me, "I had never heard that term 'Cosmic Christ' before you used it in your talk, but now I'm going to go around talking about the 'Cosmic Buddha.' It really works for me."

In Section Two of this book, Bishop Marc Andrus compares the Tibetan Buddhist mandalas to ancient paintings of the Christ Mandala. This, too, is a celebration of the interfaith dimension of exploring the Cosmic Christ archetype. Consider, too, the ancient Hindu teachings from chapter 10 of the Rig Veda about the Prajapati who was the "Cosmic Man," a Primeval Man (Purusa) who existed before the beginning of the Universe and who was sacrificed but survived his own dismemberment. He represented the Order of the Universe in tension with the chaos of the Universe. Does this not sound very much like the "Logos" celebrated in Station One but also the Crucifixion (dismemberment) that is also included in the Nativity Station and the Baptism Station (out to the wild and chaotic wilderness) and the Transfiguration? We are told that the unity of the world is based on the concept of the Cosmic Man.

These are the times we are living in. Humans are being shocked out of our anthropocentrism or narcissism as a species, and out of our tight religious boxes, in order to see the larger context of our lives and the marvelous diversity of cultures and religions amidst the beauty of the vast universe. We have seen ancient teachings from indigenous people, from Hinduism, from Buddhism, and from Judaism that speak powerfully to a sense of an "image of God," a god-like nature, a "cosmic man" not unlike the archetype of the Cosmic Christ. Mystics from varied traditions have more in common than we have been told.

We are hopeful that the practices and meditations we share here of the Cosmic Christ might catch fire and assist our species' evolutionary growth out of smallness and to the return of the mystery of the sacred cosmos. Such a leap can set humanity on new—and simultaneously more ancient—journeys. That is our prayer for this book of prayers.

There is something very revolutionary about this book—and it is not that the classical Stations of the Cross are being balanced (finally) with the Stations of the Cosmic Christ, though that is a necessary shift in theology and spiritual practice. What is so revolutionary in this book is the outreach to science and cosmology and ecology—long overdue and utterly lacking in fundamentalist, anthropocentric, and narcissistic religion and psychology ("narcissism" is a word rightly invoked by Pope Francis on numerous occasions when speaking of our cultural times). A shift to Cosmic Christ consciousness is a shift away from preoccupation with life after death to a commitment to life before death and a shift away from crass materialism to a renewed sense of sharing and community and reverence and respect. A shift away from isolation and cosmic loneliness that anthropocentrism breeds to a sense of a living cosmos, an alive universe and an alive Earth begging for us to wake up before it is too late. If "ecology is functional cosmology," as Thomas Berry teaches, then a Cosmic Christ viewpoint is a necessary prelude to an ecological awakening.

A second revolutionary dimension to this book derives from its radical ecumenical and universalist and nonsectarian dimension. While it deals with the concrete and historical realities of the life of Jesus, his teachings and those who experienced him during and after he died, it does so in a context that is not about any particular religious tradition. Why is this so? Because all the great religions of the world, when examined from their deepest mystical perspective, speak to the archetype of the Cosmic Christ. As I said in my original book on this topic, *The Coming of the Cosmic Christ*, there is no such thing as a Roman Catholic rainforest, a Buddhist ocean, a Lutheran sun, a Baptist moon, or an atheist cornfield. Once one puts our diverse religious traditions into a proper context—that of creation itself—all find some humility and all find anew their relationship to each other.

You put the first revolution and the second revolution together and you have two radical shifts, shifts away from anthropocentrism to ecology and cosmology on the one hand, and a shift away from religious isolation and competition on the other. You have a revolution therefore. What is left after these fundamental shifts?

What remains is the sacredness of all beings—whether the microcosm of individual beings or the macrocosm of the universe itself still birthing after 13.8 billion years of unfolding and gestation. How important is that, the return of a sense of the sacred? A dream told me years ago that "there is only one thing wrong with the human race today: You have forgotten the sense of the sacred." Only one thing wrong with us—how shall we cure it? What is the medicine? The Cosmic Christ, Buddha Nature, Primordial Man, Image of God, Great Spirit, assist us to cure it.

And so does the practice of the Stations of the Cosmic Christ, because humans need practices to stay on a path.

THE ARTISTS SPEAK ABOUT THEIR WORK

The two artists whose work graces these pages are M.C. Richards and Ullrrich Javier Lemus. Each has spoken about their work depicted here, and these insights will be cited alongside their icons. Each has also spoken in general terms about the artistic and spiritual journey they undertook while giving birth to their tablets.

M.C. RICHARDS

M.C. Richards, who created the "I Am" tablets, wrote about her inspiration and the journey her "I Ams" took. She tells us that they came to her unplanned and unexpectedly. They were a great surprise.

> The seven "I Ams" came as a surprise, because they weren't at all planned ahead of time. They are inspired by the imagery of what is known as Christ's seven "I Ams": "I am the Light of the World." "I am the Door." "I am the Vine." "I am the Living Bread." "I am the Good Shepherd." "I am the Resurrection and the Life." "I am the Way, the Truth, and the Life." It's odd that these sayings should have been so alive in my unconscious that they came forth unbidden. I enjoy a religious temperament and the religious cultures of the planet, but I was never a diligent churchgoer. How did they come about?

She relates the story of how, in 1964, the year her first book *Centering in Pottery, Poetry, and the Person* was published, she became very ill and had to "suffer major surgery both of my body and of my emotions." During her recovery, she was given a small booklet titled *Meditations* by Friedrich Rittelmeyer. The heart of the book was the seven "I Ams" of John's Gospel, and during that time, M.C. says, "I received a great nurturing and healing."[10]

Five years later, musing at her desk and staring out the window at the community farm where she was living, M.C. thought she would go make an image in clay of the door. Which she did. Then the other images tumbled out of her as well, all in a period of about 24 hours. "So there they were, the seven 'I Ams.' I fired them and had no idea of their future or what would become of them. I took them around with me, showed them on any number of front lawns, on the running board of my car, whenever life offered some kind of place for them."[11]

One such place that offered itself was the Episcopal Cathedral of St. John the Divine in New York City, where, quite by chance, M.C. sat next to Reverend Dean Morton's wife at a gathering and happened during their conversation to tell her of her plaques. Dean Morton was most enthused and invited her to hang them at the Cathedral, where they dwelled for six months. Later, they returned for two more years. Then they hung at my University of Creation Spirituality in downtown Oakland for nine years. And now they are on display at Grace Cathedral under the sponsorship of Bishop Marc Andrus.

On another occasion M.C. told the story of the birth of her tablets this way:

> One evening at the farm, I went to the studio to follow an impulse to work with "Door." I made a slab and a low relief spoor with a doorknob, which made me smile. I am refreshed by the ordinary in the extraordinary. The Door—the "hinge"—swinging between the worlds of sense and supersense; an opening and a pathway and a guide. I continued to work and in a few hours (or days?) had made all seven "I Ams," those images Christ had named and which I found so interesting to think of as names for one's SELF.[12]

What she is saying is of profound importance. The "I Ams," like other expressions of the Cosmic Christ, represent the large Self (as distinct from the mere ego) that connects to the one Self or Creator. It is in us all. We are all other Christs; therefore the "I Am" imagery applies to each of us. This book and the practices it contains are meant to elicit that SELF in fuller and fuller dimensions so that it takes root in our worlds of work, citizenship, family, and community building. M.C. tells us that the icons we reproduce here were born of her intuition: "Making the 'I Am' plaques … might be called an intuitive act, as it is with things I make out of a sense of ritual or seasonal festival."

In addition to being a potter and a painter and a poet, M.C. Richards was a philosopher in her own right. It seems to me that some of the teachings she shares with us impact our understanding about the icons we present in this book and how to pray with them. One day a nine-year-old girl brought M.C. an object resembling a curved plate to be fired in the kiln. "What's that, Lisa?" M.C. asked the girl.

"It's art," Lisa said solemnly.

M.C. comments:

> Obviously, I've never forgotten that moment. It was an epiphany, a revelation. From the mouths of babes … Matter that bears spirit into the fire to be transformed: It's art. How did she know that? It was, I believe, a totally intuitive, innocent, unselfconscious, essential wisdom. And it came from a deep, innocent, unselfconscious, essential source, an essential Self. This essential Self, I believe, belongs to each of us, and is at the same time a network, a basis of communion: my self and the Self.[13]

M.C. adds: "When we are in touch with this stillness and this voice, we are authentic. It is our gift and it is therefore what we have to give. We have a gift to give to one another, and we have therefore to be receptive, to be able to receive one another as gifts."

> What then does authenticity mean? She proposes the following:
> That we must live and express to one another our intrinsic mysticism, our imagination. And we want to do this in order to express the world to one another in wholeness. Not only the shard, but the art of it. Not only the clay, but the spirit of it. And our imagination is a kind of sense organ that perceives the spirit as it lives in material sheaths. It perceives and it creates: Imagination creates images, and it makes a difference what these images are, what they do. It makes a difference if they come from the essential Self, the networking self that carries life and truth that carries authenticity.[14]

M.C. Richards detects a special relationship between images and the awakening of the "essential Self," at the same time that she calls for a new marriage of "inner and outer." I think her observations parallel well the deeper meaning of a return of a Cosmic Christ consciousness—one that marries the macrocosmic world with the microcosmic world and marries the large Self within us all with the great Self of the universe—the cosmic person and what Einstein called for, a "cosmic religion" that goes beyond nationalities and tribes and other ego projections. One that brings outside and inside together again. Indeed, M.C. decries the soul loss that occurred when cosmos and psyche, science and religion, split apart in the 17th century:

> The ordinary so-called science and so-called religion of our day, in the civilization of the West, tend to conduct a cold war of their own. They attempt to co-exist and to divide the world between them. There is palpable disunion. This split obstructs the poetic consciousness; it is a characteristic malady of our society … The inner soul withdraws, goes underground, splits off from the part that keeps walking around. Vitality ebbs. Psychic disturbance is acute. Suicide may be attempted.[15]

M.C. also offers her medicine when she teaches, "Love is fostered by a capacity to experience cosmos."[16] Is it any wonder that her wisdom found so rich an expression in her tablets on the "I Am" statements of the Cosmic Christ? And that her tablets speak to a deep place in all who ponder them? Often she would travel to offer workshops around the archetypes of the seven "I Ams," encouraging people to put them into clay or color or poetry, often with powerful results.

ULLRRICH JAVIER LEMUS
THE ARTISTS SPEAK ABOUT THEIR WORK

Ullrrich Javier Lemus grew up in El Salvador during the difficult times of the Contra War and the murder of Archbishop Oscar Romero by the military. As a young man, he won awards for his sculpture and painting in his homeland, and in his early twenties moved to San Francisco, where he readily felt at home.

Ullrrich offers his reflections on his process of creating the tablets of the Cosmic Christ Events:

- Most of my pieces manifest an Indigenous heritage. Some of them look very ancestral, very old, or just came about naturally when I formed them or made them. I never did sketches or anything—they just came from my mind directly, and always with curves, influenced by my indigenous ancestry and also influenced by nature itself, by the shape of the stars or the shape of the plants or the animals who I love so much too.

- But the most important thing is everybody has their own interpretation and has their own point of view, so I see it one way but a viewer might see it another way and somebody else can see it in an even different way. So that's the thing. If they are surrealistic pieces they don't need to mean any one thing, nothing specific. I just give a little highlight on the subject. Each individual has their own experience, so each individual will have a different interpretation—so for some people it can be scary; for other people, it can be very pleasing.

- My purpose in these pieces is that everybody sees different things, whether animals or shapes or plants—I expect diverse interpretations. That's the thing with surrealistic pieces—your imagination can fly. You don't have a specific point to begin or to end. That makes it more playful … One day maybe you see one thing, and the next day, depending on how you feel or how you are or even where you are, you see different things. So that's the point of these surrealistic pieces.

I commented to Ullrrich that he presents God in many expressions here—as eye, as human, as bird, as dragon, as snake, etc. Regarding God as eye, I observe that Meister Eckhart says, "The eye with which I see God is the same eye with which God sees me." The eyes are also a sign of wisdom.

Ullrrich responded:

> Yes, the eye to me is the window, like everybody says, of the soul, of life. Eyes represent our life, our way of seeing the world, our consciousness. They are full of expansiveness. The eye is very important in the human being, how you see, what you see. And that's why I always represent God by the eye. I think it's a very good expression of Divinity.

At one point Ullrrich explained that he once had a very transcendent and powerful dream of God as a dragon. Responding to his image of God as dragon, I said, "I like the fact that your dragon, as a God figure, is wild, because I've often complained that we've domesticated God. We made God over into our image, instead of recognizing the universe is wild, life is wild, and therefore the Creator must be very wild! And I'm glad that your dream about God was about the wild side of God. It gives us permission to get more in touch with our wildness and settle less for security."

Ullrrich said:

> You know, God is not boring. God is exciting, God is not tangible. Nobody can know—it's a mystery. It can be anything, it can be many things. It's not one stipulation. It's not what the Roman Catholic Church says, 'This is God on the cross.' So I try to be more imaginative, I try to use more imagination and my creativity, which after all comes from God, not from me. It's part of him. I consider my creativity part of him. I don't consider I am doing it as if, 'Oh, I create it.' No, I'm not doing anything. I'm just a vehicle, I'm just a little object of his. I am a medium of God's creativity. God is the blood and I am the vein or channel.

We reproduce the artists' reflections along with each of their specific tablets. Unfortunately, M.C. Richards died in 1999, and I could only find specific comments from her on three of the icons. Thus I have taken it upon myself to cite other reflections from her works that seem to speak to the meaning of the remaining four "I Ams."

We are grateful for the deep contributions of M.C. Richards and Ullrrich Javier Lemus in launching this movement of the Stations of the Cosmic Christ, and we invite other artists to get on board. Already, Paola Pisani and Maciej Bielawski in Verona, Italy, have responded to our invitation; Paola has produced a series of the 16 stations in clay and Maciej has painted a beautiful icon that contains all 16 stations. We reproduce Maciej's icon and a few of Paola's stations near the end of this book, with their kind permission.

ARTISTS AND THEOLOGIANS COMING TOGETHER

It is of special meaning to us to be working with artists M.C. Richards and Ullrrich Javier Lemus in this project. Obviously we cannot do it without them. In the 1980s I visited my mentor in Paris, Père M.D. Chenu, for the last time, when he was 91 years old and mostly blind. It was he who had named the creation spirituality tradition for me when I studied with him in 1968, and as we said our goodbyes, he put his arm around me, looked me in the eye, and said with great vigor as he shook his finger: "Never forget! The greatest tragedy in theology of the last 300 years has been the divorce of the theologian from the artist, the painter, the potter, the dancer, the musician, and the filmmaker."

I have never forgotten that moment and have practiced this truth for a very long time, integrating it into all my educational work over the past 40 years. I have hired artists to teach "art as meditation" classes wherever I create spirituality programs. This book and this project is no exception. It has been a moving experience to work with the clay "I Am" tablets of M.C. Richards as well as the Cosmic Christ Event tablets as they emerged from the hands and imagination of Ullrrich Javier Lemus. Art takes us to places deeper than words alone. Art and silence are, after all, the only appropriate languages for mysticism that we humans possess.

A number of years ago, while studying the miracle and grace that we call "soil" (a gift that is rapidly disappearing and that we all depend on for our survival and yet can easily take for granted) I learned this lesson: A sign that soil is still healthy is when the birds are still around. When the birds exit and their songs are no longer heard, the soil is probably quite dead.

I can apply a parallel statement to artists and religion. Artists are the birds singing happily, and when artists are still around, church is still nourishing a healthy soil for feeding the soul. But when artists exit and no longer feel welcome in church, religion is most likely quite contaminated and possibly dead. By uniting a Cosmic Christ theology and a spiritual-religious practice via the gifts of artists, this project of the Cosmic Christ Stations represents an awakening for religion and a livening of spirituality. Grace Cathedral has often welcomed artists in its storied past, and this event is one more example of that important tradition.

It is for this reason that we sound the invitation for other artists the world over to do the same, to share your versions of the Stations of the Cosmic Christ, and for churches to extend generous invitations to artists to step up and teach us.

How many works of art through the centuries have been inspired by the great stories named here in the Stations of the Cosmic Christ? What would Western art be like had there been no stories of the Nativity, the Resurrection, the Crucifixion? The marriage of art and theology is not peripheral to our quest for wisdom; it is at its core. In fact, my book *The Coming of the Cosmic Christ* was partially inspired by my visit to an exhibit of M.C. Richards' "I Am" tablets in Carmel, California, years ago.

We are happy to encourage other artists the world-over to listen to the Spirit working in them and also give birth to the deep and playful meanings of the Cosmic Christ, the Buddha Nature, and Image of God in our midst. There is no substitute for rediscovering the presence of the Divine within and among all peoples and all creatures. When that happens in a deep manner, profound change is on its way, for we will have rediscovered the sacredness of all being.

Art takes us beyond religious tribalism and one-upmanship. This book speaks to deep ecumenism and interfaith spirituality, as the Tibetan Buddhist experience of mandala is presented in Part Two, and the Native American experience is recalled not only in the story and totem pole of the Cosmic Christ reproduced on page 198 but also in the shamanistic dimension particular to the work of Ullrrich Javier Lemus (whose ancestry is indigenous as well as Spanish).

Consider the role of the birds in both the Baptism and the Pentecost icons. The bird is a sacred messenger between the worlds of the heavens and the earth, and this is recalled in the Gospels as well as among ancient traditions that honor the eagle, the condor, the wild goose, or the dove.

MATTHEW FOX AND BISHOP MARC ANDRUS

WALKING THE STATIONS OF THE COSMIC CHRIST

Following each of the Stations is a recommended practice for walking that particular station; one is encouraged to create one's own practice as well. There is no one way to walk and pray the Stations of the Cosmic Christ. Here we will present several possibilities, and these in turn may spark one's own prayerful imagination to create one's own particular way.

1. One may want to walk the Stations by focusing (since all prayer is about focusing, after all) on the particular images the artists have created. One may do this by simply opening oneself up to the image and letting it speak to you. Ask Spirit what it is telling you and what you need to hear. Ask Spirit to invite the artist to speak to and through you.

2. Another approach is to focus more directly on the Station itself. What does the Nativity mean to you today? Or the Fireball in "In the beginning?" Or the Transfiguration? Or a particular "I Am" saying? … And so forth.

3. Another approach is to read one or both of the meditations being offered on these Stations by Bishop Marc Andrus and Matthew Fox. Often these reflections raise questions that may seem pertinent to you and your current spiritual journey. Often they contain information and reflections that may trigger an insight or response in you. Play with that insight, let it speak to you. Ask questions of it.

4. Another approach is to heed what the artists say about their work. What resonates with you, awakens something in you, lights a spark in their words as well as in their images?

5. M.C. Richards speaks in the Introduction to this book of how the "I Am" sayings of the Christ are true for all of us in our deepest self. The SELF comes alive as we give it our attention in walking these stations. Thus these sayings of the Cosmic Christ can be addressed this way as we will see below. The "I Am" applies to one's deepest and truest Self. That is key to practicing these icons.

If M.C. is correct that "love is fostered by a capacity to experience cosmos," then surely this book and the walking, talking, and prayer that derive from it represent a rebirth of love. That is our hope.

Easter 2016

PART ONE
16 STATIONS OF THE COSMIC CHRIST

1. "In the beginning was the ... Word ... Fireball ... Flaring Forth ... Big Bang ... Void ..."

ULLRRICH JAVIER LEMUS: I started beginning with nothing, and then I made the figure in clay. It's all blue with stone color and some gold colors, especially the eyes, which represent God to me. The eye is gold—it might stand for the original fireball. The round forms represent the universe—the way God tends to form things. And the forms are egg-shaped because the universe is in formation; it is coming to be like an egg. This is *numero uno*, the number one piece because in the beginning there was nothing but the fireball.

The mouth is open, blowing the breath of life. There are many curves because that is feminine and because organic forms are always curves, whether in animals or plants. All of nature operates that way—in curves.

FOX: None of us were at the beginning, though all of us are curious about it. As African-American Christian mystic Howard Thurman puts it, "It is natural that man should concern himself with beginnings. This is a part of the curiosity of the mind. Without it there would be no exploration of the world and there would be no growth … This is an inherent characteristic of mind; it is not unique to any particular age of man, culture or society. Contemplation concerning origins is a part of the curiosity of the race."[17, 18]

Today's science is learning more and more about the origin of our universe. Whether we call it the "Big Bang" (which it was not—it was silent), or the "Fireball," or the "Flaring Forth," it is all very awesome to learn that our planet's beings and the beings of every other galaxy were born in the original fireball. We were all "In the beginning …," and we all share the common atoms that were birthed in the original fireball and subsequent supernova explosions.

Before today's science uncovered these mysteries, all the world's traditions had their own stories of the origin of things. In the Hindu tradition we learn that "In the beginning was the sound," and in aboriginal stories we hear that the beginning was "the Dreamtime" in which every creature was sung into existence with its own unique song. Among Native American traditions we learn a great variety of what was "In the beginning"—a dream; silence; darkness; water; nothing; a lone woman in a cave; the beaver, and much more.

In the Bible we have many creation stories. Genesis One says in the beginning was the Void or the Dark Waters. The Book of Proverbs says that even before the beginning there was "Wisdom playing with God." John's Gospel says that in the beginning was "the Word" or *Logos*, which is also Wisdom, and which is also the Cosmic Christ.

The Cosmic Christ was at the beginning, and it has always been with us, nurtured us, summoned us, and intended us; it has always been preparing for us. The mystics have known this. As Julian of Norwich put it, "We have been loved from before the beginning," and, "God never began to love us."[19] Mechtild of Magdeburg also said, "From the very beginning God loved us. The Holy Trinity gave itself in the creation of all things and made us, body and soul, in infinite love. We were fashioned most nobly."[20] Meister Eckhart says that for us to return to our beginnings is to return to God, because God is "always in the beginning," and in that sense God is always young and always new. Indeed, the "newest" thing in the universe is God. And this is the reason, he maintains, that both the Hebrew Bible and the Christian Bible (Genesis and John's Gospel) begin with the important words, "In the beginning."[21]

The light that today's science sheds on our beginnings is awesome and potentially sacred. It can stir us to wonder and gratitude and reverence again, and ignite fresh discussion about our common origins, our holy beginnings. Such a discussion is necessarily a discussion about the Cosmic Christ (or Buddha Nature) who is always at the beginning and was "In the beginning." But the Cosmic Christ is also now and in the now. As we learn to be more present to the now we are also in our beginning again. We are fresh, and young, and new; ever reborn, ever new.

To meditate deeply is to return to our origin, to our source. Meister Eckhart says it is to return to our "unborn self."[22] Imagine that! We are capable of returning to our radical self, our unborn self, our utterly free self, before any knowledge or any choices were required of us. That taste of non-self or pre-self or unborn-self gives us immense energy and freshness to face life every day as a newborn Cosmic Christ, a bearer of Wisdom, a son or daughter of Wisdom—an incarnation of *Logos*, of the Godself. For that is who we are: the Cosmic Christ being born.

It follows then that however humans of the past or of today talk about our common origins, one thing is certain: It is a sacred story. A story that moves us all, for it connects us to our ancestors in the deepest of ways, in the holiest of ways. We need to honor, to render ceremonial, and to remember those stories, and also to ask how the language of our ancestors speaks loudly to the stories of today and vice versa.

BISHOP MARC: The Great Flaring Forth—relationship is at the heart of it all.

"In the beginning was the *Logos*, the dynamic, creative pattern of love" (John 1:1). And from that point, the Great Flaring Forth, all things emerged from the fire. Indeed, it is true to say that all meaning emerges from the fire in the Great Flaring Forth, for the meaning of all things is not separable from the totality of all that is. But in our encounter with the Archetypes of the Cosmic Christ, the first discernible meaning, lying within that initial instant, is the focus: All things in the universe are related to one another.

All things are indeed kin, born together and consisting of the same cosmic matter, interwoven with Time, another child of the Great Flaring Forth. When encountering the Archetype of the Great Flaring Forth, then, it might be the right time to ask about how you are relating to "All Your Relations," as the Lakota people put it.

Particularly because we are only very slowly waking up from a fantasy that humanity exists apart from all the rest of life, a fantasy that we exist in and on—but not of—the environment, it might serve well here to take stock of all your relations who are otherkind.

Drawing on the work of cosmologist Brian Swimme, Dominican Sister MacGillis created a ritual way to enact the 14-billion-year history of the universe. A rope spiral is laid out on the floor or ground, its length being calculated to be in proportion to 14 units. At the very center a large, beautiful candle is placed, representing the Great Flaring Forth, the Big Bang. Smaller votive candles are placed at intervals along the spiral, representing key moments in cosmogenesis and development, such as the birth of stars or photosynthesis.

As one person reads from *The Universe Story* by Brian Swimme and Thomas Berry, another, the Cosmic Walker, lights each candle, beginning with the candle of the Great Flaring Forth. While the Great Flaring Forth candle is being lit, the Reader says, "How you tell the story of the beginning makes a difference." She goes on to say that Woman could emerge out of the fire first, or Man, or Wolf, and in each case the story that radiates out from that beginning is different, unique.

WALKING STATION 1. "In the beginning was the ... Word ... Fireball ... Flaring Forth ... Big Bang ... Void ..." Which of these namings of our origins speaks most directly to you?

How does it feel to know that you were part of the origin of the universe 13.8 billion years ago (since we now know the whole universe began at that pivotal nanosecond)? Can you feel, as Hildegard of Bingen said, a new sense of being "wrapped in the arms of the mystery of God," or of realizing anew what it means to say along with Hildegard that, "It was love which was the source of this creation … The whole creation was formed through love … Love was the first … Love was in eternity and brought forth, in the beginning of all holiness, all creatures without any admixture of evil. Adam and Eve as well were produced by love from the pure nature of the Earth"?[23] Can you truly grasp what Julian of Norwich said when she declared, "We are loved from before the beginning"?

What difference does this understanding make in your life? What wounds does it begin to heal?

> "O Spirit, teach me anew and in the context of a new universe story what it means that all of creation, myself included, was 'loved from before the beginning.' Teach us what it means in giving new life and meaning to our struggling species today."

2. *"I Am the Light of the World."*

M.C. RICHARDS: The angel sips at our toes, drinks us in. Rolls us into the sun and we rise shining. How do we remember what it is to be human persons?[24]

The Christ Within: what a beautiful thought! The warmth and light and love radiating from within …[25]

llumination grows within us, sometimes like a swift mutation, sometimes like the yellowing aura of spring. But most readily it comes if we give up all that we have in order to be open-souled when it comes. That it may take its shape whole in us.[26]

BISHOP MARC: Light in John's Gospel is truth and love. Truth is our deeply interconnected reality; love is self-giving love in this matrix of interconnectivity.

Night and light shape the Gospel of John and provide the either shadowy or illumined container in which all the events of that Gospel occur, and within which the archetypes of the "I Ams" are manifested.

Both light and night are supernatural qualities in John's Gospel. The latter is ignorance of the truth … but what truth? Truth in this sublime gospel is the Unity of God that holds all beings together. Night, the converse, is the delusion that we are separated from one another, from the Earth and from God.

Love arises naturally from the Light of the Truth, as hatred is the product of the delusion of Night. The two symbolic systems of "Light and Truth and Love" and "Night and Delusion and Hate" seem to be polar opposites, not connected to one another. However, in our lives it is such that, "The Light shines in the darkness, and the darkness cannot overcome it." The two are in relationship with one another throughout our lives.

In fact, rejecting the shadow realm is precisely to buy into the delusion of separation that comes with Night.

Rather, we are invited to follow the path of the Cosmic Christ in John's Gospel. Jesus lovingly teases Nicodemus when he comes to him under cover of night at the inception of the Gospel, and Jesus also allows Judas to embrace and kiss him in an act of betrayal (enveloped in night) at the end of that Gospel.

When you come before the Archetype of the Cosmic Christ as the Light of the World, you may wish to reflect on how the overlighting, while not able to be overcome by Night, instead lovingly embraces all that lives in the Night, ending fear, confusion, and isolation. The spiritual challenge in this Station, "I am the Light of the World," might be to overcome the duality of light and shadow and absorb the truth of the psalmist's verse: "Even the darkness will not be dark to you; the night will shine like the day, for darkness is as light to you" (Psalm 139:12).

What needs to be brought into the Light of God's love in you, in your world?

FOX: Science says that the "fireball" or "flaring forth" was the first event of the birthing of the universe. Genesis teaches that light was the first act of creation. The Christ is spoken of as the "light of the world" and Jesus instructs the rest of us be "lights of the world" who do not "hide our light under a bushel but put it on a lamp stand for all to see" (Matthew 5:15f).

This teaching from Jesus derives, of course, from an era with no electricity and minimal light sources from the time the sun went down to its rising the next day. Light was ever so precious and rare and sought after. But we—you and I—are lights of the world.

The Buddha said, "Be a light unto yourself." In what ways do we have to evolve to be light to ourselves?

The Christ in all of us, the Buddha nature in all of us, provides the Light and the Shining, the direction inside the dark where we all struggle.

This Cosmic Christ saying also implies that we deal with our own darkness—all the unfinished business, shadows, and things we fear to face in ourselves need to be pierced by light and by truth. We have to come out of the shadows to face the light, and even choose to shine the light on the unwanted, unknown, or in-denial parts of ourselves. Otherwise we are not a clear light in our sharing and offering to others.

Consider this recent letter I received from a seeker. She writes: "And now the processing begins. I'm SO terribly tempted to launch into a session of beating myself up for being such a hermit and NOT getting out there and helping everyone in sight … NOT having an outside job, NOT going to the wonderful gatherings of the wonderful progressive groups that I support online … There's a horrible dark inner monster of self-contempt and fear and inadequacy and belief that I won't fit in, and confusion and wondering where the **** I'm supposed to go, what the **** I'm supposed to be doing and … just feeling scattered and scared and completely useless … And ALONE." Clearly this person is in need of seeing anew the light within herself and learning from others that there is a light within each of us.

> In what ways are we Light to others?
> Light makes learning possible.
> Light warms.
> Light awakens—thus the term "enlightenment."
> Light illuminates, opens us up, disarms us, brings transformation. Thus, Hildegard of Bingen painted her visions and called them "illuminations."
> Light stands up to depression. And to cynicism. And to boredom or couch potatoitis or acedia.
> Light transforms the darkness and radically changes it; light displaces darkness.

Today's science has broken through age-old basic dualisms of spirit versus matter, light versus darkness, when it declares that all matter is "frozen light." Light is the most common and universal synonym for the Divine that we find in all spiritual traditions around the world, from Buddhism to African religions, from the Celtic tradition to Hinduism, from Islam to Christianity.[27] By declaring the Cosmic Christ the "light of the world," something is being said about the omnipresence of the Divine in all beings, in all photons, in all atoms of the universe, in all matter. This is truly incarnation at work. The Divine becomes enfleshed in matter and in light (which is ultimately what matter is). The Cosmic Christ is found wherever matter is found—which is to say, wherever light is found.

The darkness of night. How sweet and calming and welcoming it can be after the busyness of a day of lights-on at the workplace, or the hassle of a busy mind solving problems, greeting strangers, arguing with coworkers, driving in traffic, shopping for groceries, discharging the kids—all our daytime jobs.

Night comes as a relief, a time of no-thought, of rest, of needed repose. But not forever. One can have too much of a good thing, even of sleep, and the birds begin to stir … A few brave ones sing their special song right about when the day begins to dawn and the sun rises and daylight creeps through the lowered window shades.

Light moves. It waxes and wanes, recedes and returns. It comes and it goes with the seasons and the weather and the time of day. We welcome its return. We need it, deep, deep down. We know how badly we need it—for warmth, for sight and vision, for delineating all that is one in the dark but is wonderfully unique and particular in the light, for shades and nuance, for diversity's sake, for varieties of colors all speaking with their unique and singular voice … We need the light.

We need the light for eating, since we know that all food is derived from photosynthesis, which is in fact sunlight entrapped and rendered edible and delicious by the plants. All food is light. To say, "I am the light" is to say, "I am food." Without light where would we be? Not just in the dark and in the darkness but cold and hungry and lost and forgotten. Food for no one. No light, no warmth.

Light is warm; it is fire; it is needed.

"I am the light." The light in all things. The photons (light waves) in all things. The original fireball in all things. The sparks in all things. The electric intelligence in all things.

How am I light unto others?

"Do not hide your light under a bushel." How am I doing with my light? Is it engaged and on display and bearing testimony to the truth? To justice? Is it drawing attention—not to me or my ego but to the light in all things, the "light of the world?"

How to stir one another's light?

"Matter is frozen light," says the physicist David Bohm.[28] Have I imbibed this truth yet? Have I integrated matter and spirit, Divinity and matter, as post-modern science invites me to do?

The Celtic people are said to have "adored the light. Light is the mother of life. Where there is no light, there can be no life."[29] The Scriptures say God is "wrapped in a robe of light!" (Psalm 104:1-2) and the first act of creation was God saying, "Let there be light" (Gen. 1:3-5). Hildegard of Bingen calls God "the supreme fire" that "enkindles every spark of life."[30] For Meister Eckhart God "glows and burns with all the divine bliss in the spark of the soul."[31] For Buddhists, the Living Buddha is "always shining, always enlightening trees, grass, birds, human beings, always emitting light."[32] Sufi mystic Hafiz believes "our destiny is to turn into Light Itself."[33]

"Light of the world." That is lots and lots of light, for the world is a vast and ever-expanding place, and light beams in every atom in the universe.

WALKING STATION 2. How am I the "light of the world"? How am I not? How can I allow more light to shine? How is the culture I am part of a "light of the world"? How not? How can it improve?

> "O Spirit, teach us how to become a light to the world and to link up with other lights to enlighten our species in these trying times."

ULLRRICH JAVIER LEMUS: In the Nativity, I put the mother with the child, presenting her with a blessed face—she is happy, and she is tender, pleased with the fetus that starts forming in her womb. The shape of the head is like the umbilical cord, which is connected of course with the fetus. In the back are the lines, which represent explosions of life coming to be in the universe. Blood flows and life is passed on.

On the left side is a curve to represent the curve of life itself. Life never goes in one way; it always goes in different directions. The colors are pastel stone, brownish, and this mother—any mother—is happy at giving birth. The fetus might be seen as infinity, in which case the mother is a Cosmic Mother, a Cosmic Mary, mother of the universe.

In the middle of the head is a sort of leaf with veins in it. I represent a lot of organic forms in each piece; it's like a heart is in the middle of the head, too, or like a little rose forming.

There is an emphasis on the umbilical cord, which is a marvelous metaphor for interdependence. The whole universe is interdependent. Also, the face is a very indigenous face, a very ancient woman there from an ancient tribe. It's an indigenous profile—she looks like she could be American Indian, or an Indian from South or Central America or Mexico. I tried to represent that in this piece.

Putting the heart inside the head also tells an important story. To me, that means Wisdom as opposed to raw knowledge. With Wisdom, heart and head unite. And Wisdom is part of what the Divine Feminine gives birth to. This woman is very down to earth.

FOX: Scholarship has proven that Jesus was not born on December 25, Christmas Day. We don't know Jesus' exact birthday. The early Christian community chose the winter solstice time, the darkest time of the year in the northern hemisphere, to celebrate the birthday of the Prince of Peace and the Living Light.

It follows that Christmas is a remembrance of Jesus' birth, but it is also a celebration of the birth of the Cosmic Christ, the birth of all of us as the Cosmic Christ. Christmas therefore is your birthday and mine and every other person's as the Cosmic Christ, the Son or Daughter of God, the Living Wisdom, the Son of Man, the eternal presence of the Holy One. "We are all other Christs," said the Catholic monk Thomas Merton … said the great medieval mystic Meister Eckhart … said the feminist liberation theologian Dorothee Soelle … said the founder of the Catholic Worker movement Dorothy Day. We are all other Christs—your friends and relatives and your enemies. We are all other Christs. Christmas is a celebration of our birthing other Christs. In this way we are other Marys, too, for "we are all meant to be mothers of God," as Meister Eckhart put it.[34]

Our nobility and God-like origins, and our diverse natures, are being remembered and celebrated on Christmas Day.

And Jesus is being remembered too. He who so lived out and taught and modeled the divine nature that was in him; his birth as Cosmic Christ is also celebrated this day.

> The animals celebrate it at the manger.
> The angels celebrate it with praises of peace.
> The shepherds celebrate it though they be the lowest on the societal totem pole.
> The wise men from the East celebrate it—and they were "pagans" who were neither Jews nor followers of Jesus.
> The stars in the sky who assisted the wise men celebrate it.
> Jesus' mother and father celebrate it.

We celebrate it—Jesus' and your and my birth as a Christ child, a Christ child welcomed full of grace into this holy and unrepeatable but also wounded cosmos—we all celebrate it.

Let joy ring out and choirs of angels sing. "A child is born to us, a Prince of Peace, a Comforter." Us: You and me.

What does Christmas mean in the 21st century? In this tablet we see a mother birthing a cosmic figure, a Cosmic Christ. Are we all meant to be "mothers of God," as Meister Eckhart said? Are we all meant to birth the "Prince of Peace" in ourselves and our cultures—a great Light in the darkness of poverty and antagonism, of greed and war and racism? Is Nativity an archetype, a promise, of new beginnings where the Divine will be found freshly in every animal, in everyone in a lowly state—whether among shepherds to whom good tidings are announced or among the rejected of the world?

Who will bring about this New Life, this new birth, if not us? If not every ordinary citizen who is working to resist injustice and the wispy promise of consumer success in order to birth the authentic Christ child, Wisdom child, that each of us is?

If we are all "mothers of God," Mary does not stand alone. Rather, she stands (or sits or lies down) first among equals. What an announcement: the gift of our being midwives, channels, agents—even mothers— of the Divine. What amazing news! What a surprise! What an exalted role for humans—to gather the "mind of the universe," the Creating all, into human form and into human history.[35] How amazing is that? Who would have imagined? Who would have expected this from so modest, so lowly, often so broken a species as ours?

The Nativity stretches our imaginations like nothing before. How can the wisdom of a universe 13.8 billion years old and hundreds of billions of galaxies vast pour itself into human form, not once but countless times? Why would it do so? There must be a great attraction involved here, a great love. A sensitive awareness of a deep need on the part of humans to get their act together finally, to be agents of grace and compassion, of creative healing and wondrous beauty. God among us. God-with-us, Emmanuel indeed.

The umbilical cord looms large in this icon. A rich symbol of our ancestral dependence, of our ancestors' journeys, the dependence of child upon mother in human affairs. Lifeline of nourishment and nutrition and sustenance. How dependent we all were at our beginning. And interdependent in our mother's womb, as well as afterwards, when we grow up and interact with others in myriad ways.

The story of Christ's birth does not only speak of the angels and shepherds, animals and stars. It also makes mention of the evil power of the empire represented by Herod. Herod wants to kill every newborn male child in order to be saved from reform or renewal, and so that he can preserve his ego's power and his imperial mastery. The Dark Side—Crucifixion—is hinted at here (as it is in the Transfiguration event). The story of Herod and the Empire being so threatened by a newborn baby that he wanted to kill all male babies got Jesus' father Joseph to act on a dream, one that warned him to take Mary and child to Egypt to escape the Empire's clutches.

That tale of empire and threat, plus the poverty and crisis of Mary giving birth in a manger amidst the animals in the harsh cold of winter, speak to the shadow side of Jesus' life. Life was not going to be a cakewalk for Jesus or his family. No luxuries there. Then again, Jesus never said, "Blessed are the comfortable." Neither did the Buddha.

BISHOP MARC: Here the focus is on the embodiment of spiritual principles of justice and freedom in a human life—Mary's life.

Of course when we come to the Archetype of the Incarnation, it is natural that the attention is on the baby, the infant who will be named Jesus (Savior) of Nazareth. But in reality the Incarnation of Jesus is only beginning at the moment of his birth. A far more apt meditation on Incarnation can be found by turning to the baby's young mother, Mary of Nazareth.

Paintings of the Annunciation, the angel's message to Mary that she will bear (and raise) the Longed-for One, often show a shaft of light (perhaps with a dove flying down the path of the light) coming from heaven and resting on Mary.

Mary, a young woman, a whole person, with the indivisible (as Jewish theology had it) body, soul, and spirit that is characteristic of the human being, willingly receiving spiritual principles and taking them into her humanity—this is Incarnation, the spiritual becoming enfleshed.

The hymn we often call the Magnificat tells us what values Mary was making a part of herself: praise of God, humility, the embrace of justice and liberation for the poor and oppressed, faith that God stands with the poor, and that the dispossessed will be vindicated.

We can see that the child, Jesus, willingly took into his own being these same principles, received not from an angel but from his mother. When we stand before the Archetype of the Incarnation, figured as the Holy Family at the time of the birth of Jesus, it is a good time to remember our teachers. All those people who imparted to us the values and principles that guide our lives. You might ask yourself several questions about Incarnation:

> *How can I see these principles embodied in the lives of the teachers?*
> *Who imparted them to me?*
> *How have I taken these values and principles into my own life?*
> *How have I incarnated these ideas in ways differently than my teachers?*
> *What work remains to be done in incarnating the spiritual in my life?*

WALKING STATION 3. How meaningful is it that the animals and angels, shepherds and pagan wise men, stars and Jesus' parents are all involved in the birth of the Christ—wherever that happens? As it happens in myself and in my culture, in our institutions and communities and all our relations? How meaningful is it that Herod, the representative of the empire, also shows up?

> "O Spirit, lead us into a fuller recognition of the God-self and Cosmic Christ we behold in every creature, and especially the newborn ones, those beginning life with so much promise and eagerness. Give us the grace to parent them wisely."

4. Baptism

ULLRRICH JAVIER LEMUS: A great bird dominates this clay piece and it represents the Holy Spirit descending from the sky and wrapping itself around Jesus, who is present near the bottom of the piece. There is something very festive about this piece—baptism as a feast or a festival is being spoken of. It is a very happy tablet. It is playful and childlike—colorful marbles and beads are present in the very alive sky, and these represent the planets and stars that shine and smile down on us. I am appealing to children and not just adults. The piece includes having fun; freshness and spontaneity are celebrated.

It is earthy with stone colors that blend well with the stone pillars of Grace Cathedral. For two hours I baked or cooked many crystals and gold stones or pyrite—what is known as "fool's gold"—into the clay. The result is that the piece actually looks like a big cookie—a chocolate chip cookie with colorful M&Ms. What child would not be excited about that? Or what adult with the child still alive in him or her?

I see the baptism of Jesus as something festive, not solemn. After all, it is a cosmic event since we are told that the sky opened up. An explosion of colorful beads and bird feathers as colored glass dominate. Water too; much of the glass is blue for that reason. The great dove may actually have dived under the water too. The glass reminds one of the stained glass found in Grace Cathedral as well as medieval cathedrals. Maybe the bird is not a dove; maybe it is the sacred bird of North America—the eagle; or maybe the sacred bird of South America—the condor; or maybe the sacred bird of Celtic lands—the wild goose. Or a combination of all the above. Who knows?

In the sky the planets and stars of the universe, represented by marbles we played with as children, are celebrating the baptism of Christ. There is a three-in-one God depicted—the Creator (the universe); the Christ with the divine eyes we all possess looking at us; and the Holy Spirit as a great bird. But in this piece we can't get away from the fun and deliciousness of being baptized into so beautiful a creation, so colorful a cosmos full of beauty and delight. Good things await us. A little humor is welcome by God.

BISHOP MARC: Plunging into the chaotic waters; being raised, reordered.

John the Baptist predicted a truly cosmic baptism that would be practiced by Jesus the Christ, that of Holy Spirit and fire. Properly understood, however, John's own baptism is one that has cosmic dimensions. When John baptized Jesus, those dimensions came into their fullness. They represent an initiation into a fully human, fully heavenly life.

John preached a baptism of repentance. Repentance has been reduced, in accord with the Western trend of privileging the intellect and devaluing the body and the emotions, and has become what the name implies at the barest: a rethinking. Repentance prior to the modern period, though, was something that caught the whole person up, body, mind, and soul.

Indeed, the Greek word from which we get "repentance" might be well translated as "getting the new consciousness we need for our new conditions." This is a thoroughgoing process, and so while many baptisms today are done by pouring a small amount of water on the head of the person being baptized, John the Baptist baptized by immersion. In classic Greek literature, the word for baptism was used when talking about saturating something in another medium and was even used to talk about the drowning of sailors. Ritual baptism referenced death, the ending of one mode of life so that another might begin.

The waters of baptism into which the initiate is immersed represent the life that is dying. In ancient Syriac thought, the rivers and oceans were home to the primordial forces of chaos. The Baptism of Jesus, the Cosmic Christ, shows us Christ taking on the "old life" of the Cosmos, a life that we'd be happy to leave behind—division, bitterness, hatred—the destructive aspects of life. As the Cosmic Christ takes them on, symbolized by being immersed in the waters of chaos, he takes them with him into death. Jesus was being saturated in the ancient chaos so that beyond death there might be a fresh start, a new life.

It was the Holy Spirit who was the agent of Jesus' reintegration as the Christ and the Messiah, an initiation which, though it was begun by John, continued in the wilderness under the tutelage of the Spirit herself. The

Spirit descends on Jesus in the waters of baptism; the Spirit then drives Jesus into the wilderness where he fasts and faces his temptations. Baptism is a process, then: a transformation that will last throughout our lives.

The Archetype of the Baptism of Jesus is a most potent symbol—it is about acquiring a new consciousness, after all. When we encounter it, radical choices lie before us. Are you ready to have the prior status quo turned over for the needs of a world longing for a new beginning? To become an agent of new life? If you are at such an important point, pray for the appearance of a companion, a teacher, a guide—your own John the Baptist to step into the antistructure with you, and to raise you up and to point you out as a child of God.

FOX: We are told that when Jesus was baptized by John the Baptist (his mentor in his adolescent years), the sky opened up and the Spirit in the form of a dove descended on him, while a voice from heaven said, "You are my Son, the Beloved; my favor rests on you!" (Mark 1:11) We are reminded of the teaching of the prophet Isaiah, "O, that you would tear the heavens open and come down" (Isaiah 64:1).

Thus Jesus' baptism is a cosmic event: one where the sky opened up, and occurring in the wilderness where John and his disciples (including Jesus) lived, prayed, and did their inner work together for years. No doubt it was a rite of passage for Jesus—as it is meant to be for all of us. It is emblematic of a vision quest, where one's awareness is pierced through, often in dramatic fashion, and one sees the world and one's role in it in a new, important, powerful way. In such an experience one comes face to face with one's calling or vocation, and one becomes empowered to carry on the work one is here on Earth to do.

Markian scholar D.E. Nineham calls Jesus' baptism the "curtain raiser" or "prologue" to the entire Gospel of Mark. What immediately follows is the story of Jesus going into the desert, where he wrestles with wild beasts and is tempted by Satan, and where the angels looked after him (Mark 1:1-13). The Spirit is said to have "driven him into the wilderness," so here, too, we see how the cosmos sets the tone for Mark's entire Gospel. Remember, too, that in Jesus' day lions lived in that desert wilderness. It took courage and shamanistic communion with the animal world to survive there. The cosmic motifs of these stories play over again and again in the events of Jesus' life that follow from the Transfiguration through to the Crucifixion and beyond.

In what way do we undergo vision quests and breakthroughs and calls to our vocation these days? Have you had experiences similar to those that Jesus underwent? What is the cosmos asking of us? What is the Earth asking of us? Are they opening wide and calling to us? Will empowerment come with our calling, so that we can see it through as we play out our vocations in whatever manner they present themselves to us? Do we hear ourselves called "Beloved" with the "divine favor resting on us?" (Mark 1:11) How can we assist others to find their holy vocation?

WALKING STATION 4. How have I undergone vision quests or similar breakthroughs that have revealed my deep calling and purpose for being on this earth at this special time? How do I develop my courage to fulfill my calling? How have I been empowered with gifts I have cultivated in order to be true to my vocation and recognize its deeper meaning, even when its outer form may undergo change?

"O Spirit, grace me and others with the courage and generosity to respond fully to my calling and see my work and relationships in light of that vocation. Grant me flexibility and creativity also to adjust that calling as the times dictate and as the needs of my culture require."

- Let the measure of our need be earthiness: give all things simple, verdant, passionate.
- Produce in us, for us, the possible: each only-human step toward home lit up.
- Help us fulfill what lies within the circle of our lives: each day we ask no more, no less.
- Animate the earth within us: we then feel the Wisdom underneath supporting all.
- Generate through us the bread of life: we hold only what is asked to feed the next mouth.
- Grant what we need each day in bread and insight.[37]

In addition, on his last day on Earth, at the Last Supper, Jesus left another prayer, one of remembrance: "This [bread] is my body which is broken for you. Take and eat. Do this in memory of me." These words also fill out the meaning of the "living bread"—which, like the "risen Christ" or the "living Buddha," is that presence of the Cosmic Christ that endures beyond any one particular expression in bodily form.

Jesus becomes the "bread of the world" and the "living bread" to those who are hungry for such intimacy and such sustenance. The marriage of the macro and microcosmic occurs when we dine.

When is bread "living bread"? Living bread is not stale or putrid. It is healthy and hearty and contributes life to our meals and our bodies, to our tables and our conversations and our shared conviviality. Living bread assists in sustaining and celebrating life. One way to recover the holiness of bread is to fast and go without it. When one returns from a fast, the first taste of bread and food becomes a moment of great gratitude and appreciation.

BISHOP MARC: The Bread of Life archetype is the one associated in esoteric thought with the heart chakra. In the heart, bread is made by the contributions of many outside us, and the heat of love that transforms these experiences. Then the bread is broken and distributed to the hungry world. One receives back not what they gave, but something made new by compassion.

The early second-century Christian writing, the *Didache*, says this about the Archetype of the Bread of Life: "As this broken bread scattered on the mountains was gathered and became one, so, too, may your Church be gathered together from the ends of the earth into your kingdom."[38] In this brief, potent passage we see a movement out and a gathering in. Bread broken for the life of the world is given to that same world and is reunited again.

This outward scattering and gathering in takes place in the heart, the treasury of your soul. There is no given beginning or end to this process; you need not gather in before distributing, as the fullness is already among you. Equally, you may receive the offerings of those in your life-world, taking them into your heart without fear.

Indeed, we know that all sensory data is being received by us, all the time, and yet we are not conscious of most of this information. We filter out information that is not important to us, but we also ignore information that may be vital to us but that does not fit our idea of who we are.

The gathering into the heart of scattered bread is a matter of loving attention to those around us. The material we take in to our hearts, whether it is discordant or easily taken in because it is affirming to our self-images, is all the substance of bread—which the furnace of the heart produces through love of all that is.

When you encounter the Archetype of the Bread of Life, it is an opportunity to both examine what is in your heart, and to lovingly welcome new experiences and understandings into your heart, where they will become bread to be broken for the life of the world.

WALKING STATION 5. How am I living bread for others? How am I not? How can I become living bread for and with others?

"O Spirit, teach me to become living bread and nourishing food for others. Teach me to seek out others who are living bread for myself and so we can together be living bread for others. Teach me how my work can offer living bread for others."

6. The Transfiguration

ULLRRICH JAVIER LEMUS: The mirrors in this icon invite us to reflect on ourselves, and to seek the Divinity that is within us and vice versa. It is two-in-one—us and Divinity. The mirror is the most important part of this icon. The mirrors also speak to the reality that each of us is part of everything else in the universe. We carry the elements and the history of all the other beings of the cosmos in our bodies, and our minds are eager to make connections with the rest of the universe as well.

The minerals in rocks are alive and I have inserted them into the clay, for they are part of the universe and connect our daily lives to the universe's microcosmic and macrocosmic workings. My understanding of the Transfiguration is that Jesus' inner light shone; his Divinity was on display. As is ours, and that of the rocks and other beings, if we see correctly.

The shapes in this icon depict movement and transfiguration—things get shaped and undergo shapeshifting. The eye here is made of minerals; it is a gem. So, too, the divine eye emerges in a snake shape. The snake is often demonized, as in the Garden of Eden story, but here it is redeemed. The serpent is standing up; it holds an eye of God and an eye of others; there is a harmony returning. The flesh stands for all things, not just humans: at the level of flesh, all beings are equal.

The eye at the bottom represents a deer eye and the eye at the top depicts a human eye. They are equal. Our pineal gland is in the shape of an eye also. Meister Eckhart says: "The eye with which I see God is the same eye with which God sees me." The sixth chakra is the "third eye" chakra. The Egyptians loved to depict the eye in their art as well. The eye often stands for Divine Wisdom.

I am experimenting here with mixed media—not just clay—as I mix clay and minerals, the mineral world, the animal world (snakes and deer), the human world, and the Divine world. This to me is transfiguration: recovering the Divine, which is shining and radiant in all things.

BISHOP MARC: The Transfiguration is found in three of the four canonical Gospels: Matthew, Mark and Luke. John has his own version of the Transfiguration that will be taken up in Part Two of this book, under the last, nonmetaphoric "I Am": "I Am He, Jesus of Nazareth."

Jesus takes three of his closest followers up a mountain, and there he appears to them in shining glory, accompanied by two of the great prophets, Moses and Elijah, with whom he is speaking. The disciples are paralyzed with fear, and as their understandings are clouded, they themselves are wrapped in a great cloud. A voice from within the cloud proclaims Jesus to be the Son, beloved, and the disciples are adjured to listen to him. When the cloud clears, Jesus is alone, and Moses and Elijah have vanished.

It is important to know what leads up to and perhaps sets in motion this cosmic event in the story of Jesus. After Peter confesses Jesus to be the Messiah, Jesus affirms this and then tells Peter, James, and John what the content of "Messiah" really is: betrayal, suffering, death, and then resurrection. The Transfiguration is possible for the disciples because Jesus has expanded their consciousness, has blown apart what they took to be the meaning of "Messiah."

An important detail in the story is that Peter offers to make three tents, one each for Jesus, for Moses, and for Elijah, "not being aware of what he was saying." The cloud that then envelops the mountain, the three holy figures, and the disciples is described as "overtenting" them (Luke 9:34). Small tents, small containers of our consciousness, overwhelmed by a numinous overtenting cloud.

When we face the Archetype of the Transfiguration we are confronted with our need to distinguish between worldly power and the power of God. The power of God prevails, not by dominating those who resist it, but by binding itself to the lives and the history of humans. The triumph is by means of the acceptance of reality, not its avoidance or its conquest. Where is the overtenting reality in your life? You may be in it already, unaware.

FOX: The most memorable event in Jesus' life story that links the time of the Cosmic Christ with the time of the historical Jesus is the story we know as the Transfiguration event. In a nutshell, this story recalls how Jesus took three of his closest disciples, Peter, John, and James, to the top of a mountain. There, they experienced him not so much as the teacher (rabbi) and friend they knew, but as a special spiritual figure whose countenance and garment changed, and who was joined by two special ancestors of the past: Moses and Elijah, who also experienced the Divine and lived.

Here is how the Gospel of Mark tells the story. Consider the many dimensions of the Cosmic Christ that are present—glory (*doxa*), mountain, light, cloud.

> Jesus took with him Peter and James and John and led them up a high mountain where they could be alone by themselves. There in their presence he was transfigured: his clothes became dazzlingly white, whiter than any earthly bleacher could make them. Elijah appeared to them with Moses; and they were talking with Jesus.
> Then Peter spoke to Jesus: "Rabbi," he said, "It is wonderful for us to be here; so let us make three tents: one for you, one for Moses and one for Elijah." He did not know what to say; they were so frightened. And a cloud came, covering them in shadow; and there came a voice from the cloud, "This is my Son, the Beloved. Listen to him." Then suddenly, when they looked round, they saw no one with them anymore but only Jesus.
> As they came down from the mountain he warned them to tell no one what they had seen, until after the Son of Man had risen from the dead (Mark 9:2-10 Cf; Matt 17:1-8; Luke 9:28-36).

Notice, too, that while this story tells of Jesus and his garments bathed in light and a "dazzling" whiteness, it also hints of suffering to come. Indeed, it ends with Jesus talking of how the Son of Man "is to suffer grievously and be treated with contempt" (Mark 9:12). So hints of death are in the works—glory is not distinct from suffering. The Cosmic Christ is the light in all things but also the wounds in all things.

It is telling that in the Eastern Orthodox tradition, which has remained more in touch with the Cosmic Christ theology than has the Western tradition, the Feast of the Transfiguration is the most important liturgical feast of the year, bigger even than Christmas or Easter. Yet in the West, those who can even name the date of the Transfiguration event are few and far between. Why is the Transfiguration such an important feast day? It is a great Cosmic Christ event, one that links the historical Jesus to the Risen or Cosmic Christ. It stands as the "true center-point of Mark's Gospel, the revelation of Jesus' glorious and transcendent Sonship."[39]

Peter's epistle says: "It was not any clearly invented myths that we were repeating when we brought you the knowledge of the power and the coming of our Lord Jesus Christ; we had seen his majesty for ourselves. He was honored and glorified by God and the Creator, when the Sublime Glory itself spoke to him and said, 'This is my Son, the Beloved; he enjoys my favor.' We heard this ourselves, spoken from heaven, when we were with him on the holy mountain" (2 Peter 1:16-18).

There are overlaps in this story with the Baptism event (where, as we have seen, the sky also opened up and similar words were uttered), and with the Crucifixion, for there are hints of death and glory.

How do we experience Transfiguration? How do we undergo—as other Christs—so profound an experience on our mountaintops? And how do we allow such experiences to penetrate our hearts and souls and minds? How are we witnesses of the Christ in others?

WALKING STATION 6. Jesus is revealed in his inner depths as a son of God, an image of God, a Cosmic Christ. Have I come to grips yet with my inner self—the place where the son of God, image of God, and Cosmic Christ dwell? Where Eckhart's "spark that never goes out" is always burning and shining in radiant form like a jewel? Am I becoming more and more adept at seeing the same inner light in others as well as myself?

"O Spirit, teach me the deep truth of my own—and our own—God-like-ness and Christhood, and what it means for my citizenship and work, and all our relations. Speak in the fashion you choose, to remind us that we, too, are the Beloved 'and enjoy your favor.'"

7. "I Am the Vine."

M.C. RICHARDS: The idea of the vine had that sense of continuity, carrying life with continuity.[40]

> **Deep Ecology**
> Christ's blood is green
> in the branches,
> blue in the violet.
> Her bright voice
> laughs in the night wind.
> The big nova swells
> in her breast.
> Christ suckles us
> with spring sap and
> spreads earth under our feet.[41]

FOX: My experience of vines is that they are very, very durable and inventive. They can grow through sidewalks and bricks and mortar; they find avenues through doorways and very slight openings between windows. They are tough; they are strong; they endure. They will take over backyards and houses and trees (and actually choke trees) if they can get away with it. They are hard to uproot, fiercely committed to their own survival. One must keep pruning them, cutting them back, imposing order upon them.

The Cosmic Christ speaks of pruning too (John 5:2). He calls himself a vine and us the branches, urging us to "remain in me," and promises that "whoever remains in me, with me in him, bears fruit in plenty" (John 15:5).

Vines spread; they move fast and take over. They are forever growing and fecund. If Christ is the vine, then he extends like roots do into the ground, into the dark, in search of the Source where life finds its nourishment. We, too, being other Christs, are fierce beings in search of our roots; simultaneously, we are also expressing ourselves as colored leaves and branches of the vine.

Jesus and Christ are the strong, enduring, and courage-granting root that nourishes and nurtures us—we who are the branches and the leaves.

Vines are quite ordinary; they are found everywhere. We, too, are other Christs, which means we are called to plumb deep into the depths of soil and source to find our strength and endurance and fecundity. We are called to spread into other shoots and branches and leaves—our offspring—whether they be children, grandchildren, students, or others touched by our actions, so that the vine grows and grows healthy and life-giving and ever green.

> Are we as fiercely committed to life as a vine is? As strong and determined and enduring?
> How am I a vine?
> How do I find nourishment?
> How do I grow toward full expression?
> How do I undergo pruning?

Are we vines because we are beautiful, alive, generative, strong, ever-growing, ever-adapting, ever-spreading, ever bearing fruit? What is the fruit of our vine? What delights do we bring into the world—delights as sweet as grapes?

In the Hebrew Bible, Israel itself is said to be a vine. The psalmist sings: "You brought a vine out of Egypt / You drove out the nations and planted it / You cleared the ground for it / And it took root and filled the land" (Psalm 80:8-9). And the prophet Jeremiah says, "I planted you like a choice vine of sound and reliable stock" (Jeremiah 2:21). Other prophets also speak of Israel as a vine, including Isaiah (5:1-10) and Ezekiel: "Your mother was like a vine … fruitful and leafy" (Ezekiel 19:10). The vine births grapes and humans convert these to wine, which stands as a symbol—even an archetype perhaps—for the messianic times, the good times, when justice will flow like a river, and all peoples, the poor as well as the rich, will gather at a mountaintop to be fed and nourished and drink wine together (Isaiah 25:6-9).

In the early church, wine was a symbol of the people coming together. Today, wine still brings people together: There is a social dimension to wine and therefore the vine. Among the pagan religions, too, wine served that dimension of conviviality and even sacredness, since it was a great mystery just how grapes turned into wine (the fermentation process was not scientifically understood—but the results were appreciated). Wine was mysterious, therefore, and a "gift of the gods" in many cultures long before the Bible was written. One is urged not to desacralize wine by mistreatment or self-indulgence or taking for granted, but to treat it with reverence and respect. And the Eucharist meal includes taking the cup of wine and blessing it with the declaration from Jesus' Last Supper experience: that the wine is Christ's blood.

One historian of wine points out that in the cult of Dionysus in ancient Greece, and later, in the cult of Bacchus in Rome, wine was encouraged "not simply for intoxication, though that certainly happened, but for communion. Here the communion was less with one's fellows than with the earth—specifically with nature and nature's fertile power, a power literally felt in the heat of the wine one drank, a power far greater than anything fabricated by human beings."[42] Thus Dionysus or Bacchus were not just the gods *of* wine but were also the gods *in* wine. They were in the wine drunk in cities but "[he] came from elsewhere—from the hinterland, from the vine, from nature. That nature—not the cultivated nature of the vintner or merchant, but the untamed nature of the vine itself, the nature of 'spontaneous wines'—was something that the city dweller both revered and feared."[43] In addition, Dionysus was honored for his seeming resurrection—"initial life followed by apparent death, followed by new life—corresponding neatly with the life cycle of the grapevine."[44]

John's Gospel, composed around 90 A.D. (60 years after Jesus' death), includes rich and developed "vine statements." One can see how he might have tapped in to the wine and vine imagery of the Dionysian cults of the first century. Not only is the Christ found "in wine," but also the life/death/resurrection cycle found in the Jesus story also "corresponds neatly with the life cycle of the grapevine." Vines undergo life, apparent death, and new life. So do we. Thus, "I am the vine." And you are too. We all are part of a life, death, and resurrection cycle.

In the Dionysian cults, worship was sometimes of a riotous kind, sort of a Mardi Gras atmosphere. But worship also could be very peaceful, reflective, and sedentary, a gathering to pray and discuss and invoke. Early Christian worship seems somewhat parallel.

The vine represents the sweetness and bountifulness of grapes. But in Israel it also represents eschatology—the end times, the messianic times, a better future when justice will flow like a river and we will all be inebriated by life itself. Interestingly, in Islam, too, where wine is forbidden in this life, the sign of paradise will be wine. The Koran represents paradise as a garden filled with streams and fountains of wine. The righteous are guaranteed "rivers of wine" from which they can drink their fill without any hangover or drunkenness. Free-flowing wine becomes a heavenly reward.

It follows that "I am the vine" also means "I am the wine." This has Eucharistic implications as well—another example of "this is my (cosmic) body; this is the cup of the life force of the universe." The Cosmic Christ as cosmic food and drink; food and drink as the Cosmic Christ. Science agrees that all food is cosmic food.

How am I Eucharist for others?

How am I inebriation for others?

How am I grape-delicious and grape-succulent for others?

Notice the link between "I Am the vine" and "I Am the living bread." Both require some inner work, some digging, some delving in to the depths of darkness, earth, and self. As the English mystic Julian of Norwich said, "There is a treasure in the earth that is a food tasty and pleasing to the Lord: Be a gardener. Dig and ditch, toil and sweat, and turn the earth upside down and seek the deepness and water the plants in time. Continue this labor and make sweet floods to run and noble and abundant fruits to spring. Take this food and drink and carry it to God as your true worship."[45] Our struggle to plant and harvest the vine is itself our true worship.

BISHOP MARC: Identity and fruitfulness. Service.

The identification of the Christly vine with the root chakra leads to a concentration on the idea of identity for this archetype. This is true and useful, but incomplete. Christian identity is purposeful. The true vine is part of a metaphoric system that ultimately has to do with fruitfulness.

Being rooted in the ground of our being, in God, is a goal of human life, but it does not stand alone. Perhaps it could be said that it is a proximate or penultimate goal, for there is another goal, which is loving service. Our nourishment by God is for that purpose.

There is a Zen koan that speaks to this same truth: "Be an ox on the mountainside." Searching for an irrational, abstract meaning for this koan is opposite of its true meaning. The ox is a working animal, and the meaning of the koan is that the monk ought to work in service of the salvation of all sentient beings.

When we are alienated from the source of our lives we can easily become drained: tired from the exertion of doing our life work from within the available energy of our own bodies and minds. Working from within the misconception that all we have available are the resources of our known selves is a delusion that has staying power. Because we can do so much on our own steam, for some time, perhaps even for the whole of a single human life, this delusion seems true.

God is inviting us, though, to root ourselves in the infinite, and to work from this source that is unquenchable. When you encounter the archetype of the True Vine, you might ask yourself about how much energy you have. Also, how consistently do you engage in the spiritual practices that orient you to what is life-giving?

The invitation of the archetype of the True Vine is not a call to work harder, but to remember who you are, and to rest, by means of your own spiritual practices, in the refreshing power of the Divine.

WALKING STATION 7. How am I a vine? Am I a strong and sturdy and determined vine, like Jesus was, and that I am called to imitate?

> "Oh Spirit, teach me to become a vine that is strengthened by the prunings that life demands of us, and which does not wither but grows ever greener and ever stronger … and which links up with other Christs who are doing the same."

8. "Do it to the least and you do it to me." (Matthew 25)

ULLRRICH JAVIER LEMUS: In this piece I offer two profiles of men. One is blowing what appears to be round forms or whirlpools (in Spanish, *remolino*) and the other man is receiving these. They help each other or hate each other. We give out good or we give out bad in life, and whatever you send out of your mouth comes back to you. Our egos affect other people. In this case, we have to know that we're all connected and we're all embraced, and what you do to somebody else you do to yourself.

So I tried to put these ideas in this tablet. The piece demonstrates some kind of art deco influence, along with a Mayan influence in the two male profiles, and in the colors, which are also again very earthy, terracotta colors.

What you do or you say affects others, and others' actions and words also affect you in the same way. All is connected. It's about karma. If you put out good things and blow good news and try to be positive, then that will come back to you. And whatever you do to any person—to any being, not only persons, to even a plant or an animal, which can have as much importance as a human being—how you treat them will come back to you too. What you sow is what you reap.

BISHOP MARC: Matthew 25, the Judgment of the Nations

The first thing an attentive listener may notice about The Great Judgment in the 25 chapter of Matthew's Gospel is that those gathered before the One Seated on the Throne are nations, not individuals. At first we breathe a sigh of relief, but then we start to worry, for good reasons—how will WE be judged?

This scene in Matthew 25 with the Great Being judging the entire peoples of the Earth while attended by the holy angels marks a Cosmic Christ event. Christ pronounces judgment from a cosmic seat and opens for us the thought of Good being woven into the fabric of the universe. What does it mean that there is a moral content to the universe—and that a Great Being embodies that content for us?

We see the dynamics of goodness in the universe at work from the grandest scale possible all the way down to the smallest level. While a nation is miniscule in comparison to the heavenly bodies and the distances between them, the fabric of morality keeps its shape all the way down to the individual human level and perhaps to ever smaller levels of being. We remember in this same Gospel the saying of Jesus: that even a small, uncared-for sparrow doesn't die unaccompanied by God. God's justice and mercy pervades the cosmos and touches even the smallest life.

This continuity from the macro to the micro is an ancient piece of wisdom: "As above, so below." The same dynamics and essential structures are present in each level of the cosmos. Twentieth-century physics talk about this in a parallel way as the "implicate order." The implicate order may be said to be the deep structure of reality which underlies both the galaxy and the hummingbird. What if the implicate order involves some deep goodness woven in?

One of the most quoted sayings of Dr. Martin Luther King Jr. is about the fabric of goodness in the universe:

> Evil may so shape events that Caesar will occupy a palace and Christ a cross, but that same Christ arose and split history into A.D. and B.C., so that even the life of Caesar must be dated by his name. Yes, the arc of the moral universe is long, but it bends toward justice. There is something in the universe which justifies William Cullen Bryant in saying, "Truth crushed to earth will rise again."[46]

Hands-on community organizer, movement-maker, and theologian Dr. Martin Luther King Jr. was speaking a truth that he both intuited and had been taught: that the goodness he found and also worked toward at the level of human society was mirrored and sourced in the heavens.

Mathematical cosmologist Brian Swimme has written vividly about what he calls the cosmological powers, the up-and-down processes that pattern the universe at every dimension and size. The Power of Interrelatedness, or "the power of care, how the Universe responds to the other," puts forward the idea that the universe has a corrective quality that works to transform distorted complexes. There is a judging power in the cosmos, a corrective force that ends distortions brought about by the actions of humans.

So we return to the story of the Judgment of the Nations in Matthew 25. After this short journey we've been on through esoteric philosophy and new physics, we may notice, back within the story, a few differences. First, the judging, correcting power is not impersonal; while it is awesome and extraordinary, it comes through a person. We are asked to consider Christ, who holds cosmological powers but has personhood. Within this meditation we may focus on what the personhood of the Cosmic Christ offers us—relatedness with the being and beings of the universe. We are invited to see reality as a community of subjects within the great Subject, rather than as separate objects with no relationship among them other than one of use, tinged with force and violence. One of the simplest lessons of the Great Flaring Forth, as taught by the New Cosmology, is the complete interrelatedness of the universe. Interconnectedness applies not only to planets, stars, and galaxies, but also to the living beings of the Earth. Our lives are interrelated.

We may also notice that while it is nations that are being judged, individuals speak in dialog with the great judge. The voices in dialogue with the great judge in Matthew 25 represent collective voices. Thus, while people in the Bay Area of California, for instance, are far ahead of much of the United States in living sustainably upon the earth, this has not exempted us from the responsibility for the yawning inequity between our country and many other poorer countries. Californians can't appeal for approval from the great judge on the basis of our localized goodness. We bear the responsibility of what is now being called the Anthropocene Age (a period in which human action is responsible for planetary changes) together, and we now know that "together" means all of us on planet Earth.

It is not an accident that both groups of nations overhear the detailed judgment given to each. Is this perhaps a sign of grace, that by hearing we may learn and be inspired to enter the path of repentance and transformation?

FOX: This expression of the Cosmic Christ is unique, because it is not the Christian community speaking so much as it is Jesus speaking. Jesus speaks in Matthew 25 of how when we feed the hungry we feed him, how when we clothe the naked we clothe him, how when we visit the prisoner we visit him, etc.—and this is a profound teaching about the Cosmic Christ. Jesus is not just Jesus—he is all of those who suffer and are in need. That is what the Cosmic Christ represents. In this passage Jesus is anticipating future teachings about the Cosmic Christ, most of which would develop and flow from the community after he died.

But what he teaches about himself in this passage is also true of us. We are not just "us." I am not just "me." I am you—when you suffer and when you rejoice. That is what compassion means: not that we feel sorry for each other but that we *are* one another. Ego does not have the last word.

Matthew 25 is Jesus' creative rendition of Isaiah 53, where the "works of mercy" are laid out. Both surely represent a high point in Western religion and spirituality. How are we doing with these teachings, playing and acting them out in our citizenship and work worlds, and in our families and communities?

Recently, when I was speaking on Matthew 25 at a small community gathering, a young man offered a beautiful response. He said that until he heard this teaching about the Cosmic Christ and Matthew 25 he had looked on works of compassion "as duties to be performed." Now he realizes it is not a duty. It is the way he treats himself—to be compassionate to others. A real breakthrough in consciousness occurred for him: He could move from doing "good deeds" to a more mystical understanding of ethics. With this kind of understanding, we know that we are celebrating each other's deep beauty and Christ-likeness, one another's Godliness, when we work to relieve one another's pain. And, of course, we are being so celebrated when others treat us this way, and for these reasons, as well.

This teaching by Jesus is rich and central to all of his teachings. The story is supposedly about the "end times." But in fact it is about our times, about the Now and how we could be acting right in this moment if we cared to—and if we cared to bring the "end times" into the present. It is not about life after death—it is about how to live before we die. It is about the coming of the kingdom. Therefore it is about realized eschatology—about how heaven comes to Earth now.

The entire passage is set in the context of glory (or *doxa*, in Greek). Glory is always a signal that we are talking about the Cosmic Christ, who transcends time and space and reveals the inner radiance and God-likeness of all being. The story tells how glory (or *doxa*) is let loose in the world. It is about God's kingdom (and the King or royal person we all are meant to be) in this world, not just the next.

> When the Son of Man comes in his glory, escorted by all the angels, then he will take his seat on his throne of glory … Then the King will say to those on his right hand, "Come, you whom my Father has blessed, take for your heritage the kingdom prepared for you since the foundation of the world. For I was hungry and you gave me food; I was thirsty and you gave me drink; I was a stranger and you made me welcome; naked and you clothed me, sick and you visited me, in prison and you came to see me." Then the virtuous will say to him in reply, "Lord, when did we see you hungry and feed you; or thirsty and give you drink? When did we see you a stranger and make you welcome; naked and clothe you; sick or in prison and go to see you?" And the King will answer, "I tell you solemnly, insofar as you did this to one of the least of these brothers or sisters of mine, you did it to me … I tell you solemnly, insofar as you neglect to do this to one of the least of these, you neglected to do it to me."
>
> —Matthew 25:31-41, 45

In Matthew 25 we have one of the most profound stories about compassion and about what life is all about that one will find anywhere in the world. Jesus shines here with his teaching that to clothe the naked, to feed the hungry, to quench the thirsty, to visit the prisoner, to heal the sick, is to do it to him. This very original story from Jesus that so echoes Isaiah's teaching of what we call the spiritual and corporal works of mercy is rivaled by nothing else—East or West, North or South—for telling us what it means to be a human being. Compassion is not feeling sorry for others; it is not "doing our duty" in regard to others. It is realizing that the "other"—and especially the least among us—is not other. The "other" is another Cosmic Christ, another one of us. The "other" is a subject, not an object.

One outstanding dimension to these teachings in Matthew 25 is that they come directly from the mouth of the historical Jesus. The parable depicts his moral imagination at work. Yet it is very much a Cosmic Christ teaching, and this is very significant, because as we have seen, most of the Cosmic Christ teachings came from the community itself after Jesus died. Most of the Cosmic Christ teachings are born of the sacred imagination of the early Christ community, whose spiritual consciousness was triggered by the Jesus story and teachings. But here we have Jesus himself saying, "I am not just Jesus. I am not just me. I am also you; and you; and you; I am everyone who suffers, everyone who is lonely, afraid, sick, hungry, in prison, etc." This passage in Matthew therefore is the bridge between the Cosmic Christ teachings that occurred after the death of Jesus, and the Cosmic Christ being unleashed in the very person and teaching of Jesus himself. Here the historical Jesus and the Cosmic Christ meet.

This is also a teaching about the arrival of the "kingdom/queendom of God," since the story, as Jesus presents it, takes place in the context of the coming of the Son of Man on Judgment Day. But judgment day is not so much about the end of the world as about the end of this world as we know it—the world of violence and war and neglect and reptilian brain dominance—and the beginning of another world, that of "heaven on earth," the new creation when justice will flow like rivers and all will live in peace. It is about changing this world; it is about transformation or realized eschatology; it is about the future happening in the now. It is about living "on earth as it is in heaven." It is about our times being the end times and not some future time. It is about our work while on earth.

This story gets to the deep meaning of compassion because it does not present compassion as simply a moral duty or rule or action. Compassion is a consciousness that goes beyond ego turf-building to the deep awareness that we are more than we think we are: We are one another. Your joy is my joy, your pain is my pain, your relieving of my pain is the relieving of your own pain. As Meister Eckhart put it, "What happens to another whether it be a joy or a sorrow happens to me."[47]

Notice how the word "glory" (or *doxa*), which we maintain is always a sign of Cosmic Christ awareness, is employed often in the lead-up to the teaching. Since Jesus talks about "the least" among us, this radical and basic teaching is fully applicable to the eco-justice issues of our time. To human indifference that causes the climate change and global warming that is killing species; to the release of carbon dioxide into the atmosphere; to the killing of rainforests and oceans; the poisoning of soil and waters; the extinction of unprecedented numbers of species who are so often without a voice when humans gather to make decisions about their fate in our boardrooms and legislatures. All this is news about "the least among us," for these beings are rarely represented by the rich and powerful or their multitude of lobbyists who campaign so effectively in legislatures and judiciaries. These, too, are the "little ones" who are other Christs, and to neglect them is to neglect Christ.

A brief version of this teaching is expanded on in Mark's Gospel, when we hear that Jesus "took a little child, set him in front of the disciples, put his arms round him, and said to them, 'Anyone who welcomes one of these little children in my name, welcomes me; and anyone who welcomes me welcomes not me but the one who sent me'" (Mark 9:36-37). Thus, once again, we learn that Jesus is not just Jesus (nor am "I" just "I"); but Jesus is also the little child, as we are also one another; and we are also God, the Cosmic Christ, the "one who sent" Jesus.

WALKING STATION 8. What are the implications of this teaching of the Christ in others, especially in the "least," for my calling and my work in the world? What are the implications at this time in history when so much devastation is happening on the planet amidst climate change and the extinctions of many creatures? What are the movements of justice and responses to injustice that I am part of? What am I called to be and to do?

> "O Spirit, open my heart and my ears to hear the cries of the poor and those denied a voice.
> Let me have the courage to recognize suffering for what it is and the imagination to respond to
> it in effective ways. Let me find allies, and let us change our structures, moving them toward
> community and sustainability and away from imbalance and injustice."

9. "I Am the good shepherd."

M.C. RICHARDS:

I have painted the female hills

stretched and piled against the sky

They are sleeping.

I have given them golden haloes.

They are saints.

They are sleeping.

I have painted the gold in clouds and crevices as well, meaning to say how they, too, are saints,

how the world sleeps,

how womanly is the landscape,

how a whiskered angel also sleeps as a field of grain.[48]

BISHOP MARC: This archetype is associated with the voice of the Good Shepherd. Thus, it is concerned with hearing the voice of the Divine and learning to give voice to the truth that is in us.

In the following passage from 1 Peter, we hear the letter's author encourage a group of Christians to act as shepherds by exercising oversight in their communities. He also looks forward to a time when the shepherds will themselves be tended, by the Cosmic Christ as the Good Shepherd.

> Now as an elder myself and a witness of the sufferings of Christ, as well as one who shares in the glory to be revealed, I exhort the elders among you to tend the flock of God that is in your charge, exercising the oversight, not under compulsion but willingly, as God would have you do it—not for sordid gain but eagerly. Do not lord it over those in your charge, but be examples to the flock. And when the chief shepherd appears, you will win the crown of glory that never fades away.
> —1 Peter 5:1-4

So we can see the fluidity of the archetypes: sometimes we are shepherds; sometimes sheep; never one fixed role all the time. Metaphors and archetypes can cease to serve us when they become fixed, hardened, or isolated from the symbolic system of which they are living parts. The Archetype of the Good Shepherd is a good example of the kind of metaphoric flexibility that does serve us. It also reminds us to claim our authentic voice and exercise our inherent authority. Such authority should not be confused with the will to power—it is not shouting other voices down.

When you meet the Archetype of the Good Shepherd, you may consider whether you are using your voice to its full effect, as well as whether you are being guided, defended, and cared for by the Good Shepherd. Are we tending the weakest, the most vulnerable in our communities? Equally, are we caring for the vulnerable parts of our inner selves?

FOX: The icon of the Good Shepherd is among the very oldest images in the Christian tradition. It is found sketched and painted on the walls of third-century catacombs and is depicted in statues from that era as well. It appears far earlier than the symbol of the cross, which dates back to the fourth century, and the crucifix (a cross with a person on it), which is first found in the 10th century! In the 12th century, the great mystic Hildegard of Bingen never paints the cross by itself, but only in the context of other events in Jesus' life. Yet the symbol of the cross has dominated Christianity's self-image so strongly, while that of the "good shepherd" often goes unnoticed.

What does a "good shepherd" statement mean to 21st-century people, very few of whom live and work among sheep? How am I—how are you—a good shepherd?

A good shepherd cares about his/her sheep: those who are entrusted to his or her care. Sheep need commitment in good weather and bad; they need tending; they need protection. Sheep are vulnerable. They have no armor; they are not fast runners; they cannot climb trees. A good shepherd is warrior-like—alert to the danger of wolves, mountain lions, jackals, cougars, or other predators who would harm his sheep. A good shepherd sacrifices for his sheep, allowing the sheep to dictate his or her sleeping and waking hours, break times, and fun times. Tending to sheep is a commitment: it is not a life of ease and comfort, but one of vigilance and sacrifice. A good shepherd puts the care and defense of the sheep entrusted to him ahead of his own agenda. Thus a good shepherd is not selfish but generous and giving.

Perhaps the word that best summarizes the character of a good shepherd is "steward." A good steward takes responsibility and is accountable: for one's sheep or one's soil, for one's forests and rivers and lakes, for the ocean and the air and the plants, for other four-legged creatures as well as winged and finned creatures—all of the beings we are entrusted with.

While few are called to be actual shepherds in our time, all are called to be good stewards of the earth and all her creatures. Just as the good shepherd is held accountable by the larger community to preserve the sheep, so each of us will be held accountable by future generations for how well we steward and guard and tend the beauty and health of the creation that was bequeathed to us by our ancestors. And by how bravely we stood up to the wolves of a predatory economic system and to corporate bosses and politicians who are raping and pillaging the earth and her creatures.

Am I a good guardian of the earth and its creatures? Am I working actively to defend the earth's health and that of its myriad and brilliant creatures—from tigers to polar bears, from lions to elephants, from whales to forests? After all, every creature is an "I Am," a Cosmic Christ. Myself and my species are not the only incarnations of the Cosmic Christ.

Every sheep and cat, dog and tree, lion and elephant, polar bear and river, mountain and forest, and human child, too, is a Cosmic Christ, a mystic lamb, entrusted to our care and compassion. I salute M.C. Richards' poem for its language of "golden haloes" and "gold in clouds," for she is naming the divine radiance (*doxa*) that is part and parcel of all nature. She is naming the presence of the Cosmic Christ in our everyday world. (She also painted such haloes in a number of her paintings.)

The cosmic lamb we are to protect includes the mystic lamb, the *puer* or *puella* (child) in each of us. This mystic needs protection and support in order for us to grow into the mystic lovers that we are.

The good shepherd, then, is a good parent—an adult who accepts his or her responsibility to lead and guide, to preserve and nurture, to see that the sheep entrusted to his or her care are well nourished, protected, and able to grow into healthy adults themselves.

How are we doing, we good shepherds? We good stewards? We caring parents and grandparents? We citizens of an earth filled with beautiful species, so many of which are going extinct? Are we altering our lifestyles so that we are leaving a healthy planet for subsequent generations?

WALKING STATION 9. I may not be a shepherd of sheep, but how am I a "good shepherd" and steward of the Earth and her creatures? How can I link up with others to make a difference, to defend Mother Earth and be warriors on her behalf? Am I caring as deeply about the earth as a shepherd cares about his or her sheep?

> "O Spirit, teach us the courage and trust that will allow us to stand up on behalf of those we are charged to protect—the future generations of children and grandchildren for generations to come—so that they may delight in a healthy, holy, and clean planet full of diverse plants, animals, sea creatures, and birds."

10. *"I Am the door (the gate, the way)."*

M.C. RICHARDS: The image of the door and doorway evoked a kind of archway in which one stands, something open in front and behind, a kind of hinge that swings equally in both directions … Made the door out of clay, which amused me because it was just a small door, with a doorknob I liked … It made me smile. I am refreshed by the ordinary in the extraordinary. The Door—the "hinge"—swinging between the worlds of sense and supersense; an opening and a pathway and a guide.[49]

LITURGY

> O I touch and am touched
>
> by the smouldering core of you.
>
> The colors that surface in your flesh
>
> carry my sight into the temple beyond seeing
>
> My heart is pounding, impatient for the sacrament
>
> that changes our bodies into communion.
>
> You are my door. Through you
>
> I am entered.[50]
>
> —M.C. Richards

BISHOP MARC: The door is the will shaped by love, so that it is about opening rather than closing, and moving across thresholds.

> "I know your works: behold, I have set before you an open door, and no man can shut it: for you have a little strength, and have kept my word, and have not denied my name" (Revelation 3:8).

The Archetype of the Door comes from the passage in John's Gospel where Jesus says he is not only the Good Shepherd but paradoxically, the gate to the sheepfold (John 10:8). When we hear the Ancient of Days proclaim an ever-open door in heaven in the passage from Revelation above, we begin to understand that the Archetype of the Door concerns access to the spiritual, the place of freedom and peace.

The threshold has been an important idea in all religious thought. The crossing over from one realm to another intrigues us and is also the object of intense longing for those who feel trapped or shut out. We also may fear what lies beyond the threshold, even if our present reality is one of oppression.

There are almost one billion people on Earth today who live in extreme poverty. There is a very-alive slave trade today, trafficking in women, girls, and boys for labor and for sex. Many millions of people worldwide live within the prison of addictions. All these people suffer within restrictive boundaries that they often are powerless to cross.

The third chakra, associated with the Archetype of the Door, has to do with human will. The will to cross the threshold into desired but unknown realms is the matter of the Archetype of the Door. In a remarkable moment in his play *No Exit*, Jean Paul Sartre's characters, who have been trapped in a drawing room for eternity, find that in fact the door to the room is suddenly unlocked, and if they will they can leave. In the end, no one does leave.

How do we find the courage to leave places of oppression, first in our inner lives and then by taking action with others against external oppressions? By sitting with the Door itself, whom we find to be Christ.

FOX: How is Christ a door (or a gate, or a way)? How are we a door, a gate, or a way? A door is about openings. How open are we? How much opening does the Christ accomplish in us and through us? What are we opening to? How vast are our hearts' and minds' openings? Are we opening to the universe itself? Do we let the universe into our room, into our psyche?

What thresholds open up for others because we are at work on Earth? How do we open doors and provide new vistas and new ways for others? A door is not an end in itself. A door is a temporary divider, a link, a bridge, a threshold to another world, a new opportunity—a breakthrough, even.

MATTHEW FOX AND BISHOP MARC ANDRUS

A good teacher offers a door to opening up one's mind, exercising one's brain, blessing one's talent, providing skills for learning, and using one's gifts in the world. Parents offer the same and more. Writers can do the same; artists and musicians also. When ideas liberate and excite and ignite a spark, they elicit the potential of others. Thus people who share liberating ideas are themselves doors.

A door often opens up new vistas and visions and opportunities with dreams and hopes and possibilities. All these qualities are the grace of being a door to others.

A door also protects. It keeps the cold out, and the winds, and fearsome objects and unwanted intruders. It keeps the familiar inside; keeps warmth inside. It makes intimacy possible.

A door is such an everyday thing. It welcomes one into the quiet and familiar sanctum of one's home, into that place apart from the busyness and noise of the streets and the hassle that goes on in making our living or going about our daily duties. But behind our personal door is our own home, our own place of refuge and intimacy, of quiet and relaxation. Doors protect. They guard. They make secure, as well as open up and invite new possibilities and visitors new and old.

Doors introduce what has been called "a first myth of outside and inside."[51] Do we feel outside, left out, alienated? Or are we inside, feeling welcomed, warm, protected, cozy, belonging, and at home? It would seem the Christ as door is an affirmation of belonging.

Behind closed doors there are often exciting new places to see and people to encounter. Doors entice. They fill us with wonder and curiosity. "What is behind the door?"

Yes, we are doors. We both protect and we open to new possibilities. The door guarantees intimacy but it also promises that we are not fenced in; that closeness does not have to designate closed-ness. That there is an outside to every inside; a cosmos for every psyche; for everything we know or think we know, an unknown, a surprise, a new horizon to enter, a beyond. The French poet Pierre Albert-Birot put it this way:

At the door of the house who will come knocking? An open door, we enter

A closed door, a den

The world pulse beats beyond my door.[52]

How are we doing?

How is the Christ at work in being our door?

Who is knocking at our door? How are we doors to one another?

What doors are we opening?

What doors are closing?

What is beating beyond the door?

WALKING STATION 10. How am I a door or a gate for others? Is my door open or shut? Is it welcoming or afraid? Does it house mystery and surprise or does it protect things that carry little excitement to them? Is my door a door to adventure and the deep ... or is it merely a door to make things secure and often stale? Is it balanced on its hinges? Can it swing smoothly as needed between open and shut?

"O Spirit, make of me a useful door, a door that is wise enough to know when to be open and when to be closed, when to cherish solitude and when to practice hospitality. Bless me with curiosity so that I may go hunting for the truth and beauty and greatness that lies behind the Christ doors in the world."

11. "I Am the Way, the Truth and the Life."

M.C. RICHARDS: The Way, the Truth and the Life ... is the most difficult to read, I think. It's a heart-shaped head with just a faint physiognomy, faint eyes and mouth on a rough slab background. The face is marred by the accidents of the fire; it was too close to the shelf above. When I first saw it, I thought, "Oh, it won't do." But then I thought again and it seemed appropriate that it should show signs of wear and tear. I think in a way that this piece is the most obscure because the image isn't all that clear. Also, the power of the image, heart-shaped head, and at the top of the head, the fontanelle, an opening ... What is it that can stream in? It is not close to the shelf above stone but something that is open to the influences from the spiritual world. I learned later that that image, the heart-shaped head, is an ancient image on the planet. It has been used in petroglyphs across the Pacific, toward Asia, [as far back as] 40,000 years ago.[53]

FOX: How are we a Way to others?
How are we Truth for one another?
How are we Life to one another?

We provide a way or path for others by our example of living out our values, by walking our talk, by finding a balance in our struggle between solitude and community, action and contemplation, laughter and grief, hope and despair, being and becoming, masculine and feminine, yin and yang.

Wisdom is more of a way than is knowledge or information alone. By committing to wisdom, we also embody a way that others can emulate or commit to on their own terms.

We provide truth for one another by our own open-minded and heartfelt hunting and gathering of truth. When we stand up for truth and against false powers of any kind, we are bearing witness to truth and its possibility—and that, too, is a Divine activity. In this way our pursuit of the truth of our vocations becomes truth for one another. To live out one's vocation fully, courageously, and generously is to invite others to do the same.

In what ways are we Life for one another? We are Life for one another when we put our love of life ahead of fear or control or sadness or anger. When we put life first, preferring the God of Life to the Gods of Institutions, Consumerism, Empire, and Religion. In short, when we resist false gods or idols. As Meister Eckhart put it, "Live without a why … Live for life's sake," and "I live in order to live." We drink in life, we surrender to it, we praise it, we fall in love with it daily, we sacrifice for it, we celebrate it, we fight to see that others have ample opportunities to do the same. We undergo its sometimes painful and challenging demands.

And, of course, we bring new life into the world. Sometimes this is literal life; babies require of us the vocations of parenting and grandparenting, responsible citizenship, and the nourishment of life in its multiple expressions. But there is also the more indirect begetting of life that occurs when we grow food, support living ecosystems, plant trees, love and care for animals, clean up waters and rivers and oceans, stand up for biophilia over necrophilia, teach others, and work for justice over injustice and truth over lies.

We are alive to one another when we choose to celebrate existence via rituals and ceremony which arouse gratitude and sharing, or when we birth music or dance, pots or poetry, theater or film—thus praising life as life deserves to be praised. We praise life by taking care of the old and the sick and the lame, as well as the young. We praise life through teaching and constant learning; by exciting new generations about the depth and beauty of life all around us. We honor life by studying it in its many forms. We honor it through scientific research that opens up new vistas of truth and makes breakthroughs in combatting disease, depression, or cynicism.

In these many ways (and in many more ways) we become other Christs who truly manifest the Way, the Truth, the Life for one another, and for all peoples for generations to come. This is what our ancestors, the "communion of saints," have bequeathed to us, paths to becoming the Way, the Truth and the Life. Jesus is clearly one of these ancestors, and there are many more urging us on and eager to support us.

It is interesting that M.C. Richards tells us of an aperture in the head of her icon. The seventh chakra is representative of our opening up to other light beings, and to their imaginations and eagerness to support us. Ancestors? Yes. But spirits and angels as well. All are committed to the Way of Truth and Life affirmation. Biophilia is the realm of the saints, both living and dead.

BISHOP MARC: I Am the Way, the Truth and the Life.

The waters of the primeval oceans from which our planet's life emerged, the amniotic fluid in a mother's womb that is the medium of sustenance for the gestating fetus … Life, and the unfolding path of any and all life, comes forth from water. Thus, the archetype, "I Am the Way, the Truth and the Life" indicates another "I Am," never precisely named by Jesus, but nevertheless real: that of the Living Water. Water is often a synonym for the Holy Spirit in Jewish thinking. And, of course, to desert people, water is a life-or-death matter.

The archetype of Life and Living Water directs us toward spiritual generativity as the true meaning here. There is an implicit "I Am" statement here when Jesus tells the Samaritan woman that he is offering "living water." The implication is that he is saying, "I Am the living water" (John 4:10). The Cosmic Christ archetype "I Am the Way, the Truth and the Life" leads us to think more about reproduction and generativity. "Whoever believes in me, as the Scripture has said, 'Out of his heart will flow rivers of living water'" (John 7:38). The Greek word often translated as "heart" in John 4:10 (above) would be better translated as "womb," "belly," or "gut."

Only women have physical wombs, but all humans have wombs—the loci of reproduction and generativity. All of us are called to bring forth life. You could say that everyone has a spiritual womb.

Psychologists Joan and Erik Erikson, when they themselves became elders, realized that they had not captured the heart of the developmental possibilities for elders when they had done their groundbreaking work on stages of development many years before. They came to understand that the greatest potential for the elder years is to learn how to continue to be generative.

What the Eriksons understood about the later stages of human life is true for us all when we meet this archetype. We are asked to open ourselves to be creative and generative in what may be for many of us a new field of action: the spiritual.

What new life may you help birth or parent at this moment in your life?

WALKING STATION 11. Am I a person on the Way, a person hungry for Truth and full of Life? Am I in love with life even when it throws pain and brokenness my way? Do I take care of myself so that Life and gratitude for living comes first?

> "Oh Spirit, teach me to be a lover of Life—to put biophilia first. To be a champion for Truth and a fearless hunter after it, to be a wayfarer, a pilgrim, and a traveler on life's highway. Bring people into my world who can assist me in life-loving, truth-finding, and walking a common Way together."

12. The Crucifixion

ULLRRICH JAVIER LEMUS: In this piece I put the eye, my symbol for Divinity, in the center of the cross. I shaped the cross like a starfish with curved forms and with the three divinities—Father, Son, and Holy Spirit, represented by the three forms of circles at the top. These intersecting circles can also be the mystery of Life, Death, and Resurrection. There is also a hint of a labyrinth, which represents the two labyrinths of Grace Cathedral and how important such a practice is for meditation and peacemaking. We need to remember that life begins as a spiral. And it requires water, so the curves also speak of water.

Everything here is connected once again in the shape of curves, which makes us think God is very flexible and wide. The tentacles on the starfish connect with the labyrinth.

I tried to make the cross with a little movement … it's playful, it's flexible, it's soft; it's not something rigid or strict as the cross has always been portrayed in the past. When I was a kid, I received the message that the cross was very secret, very serious, heavy religion—very intimidating. My rendering is friendlier; more appealing for me. Our symbols need fresh interpretation. My icon also represents organic form and shape.

I have learned since I made this symbol that if you cut off the limb of a starfish, a new one grows back. So there is a symbol of death and rebirth within my version of the cross as a starfish. And the cross almost looks like a bird. It wants to take flight.

BISHOP MARC: Christ didn't die because of an unalterable plan on the part of God; the necessity was internal to Jesus' life path. He chose a path that put him inevitably in the focus of a brutal imperial regime's sight. At some point he was conscious of the consequences and cost, and yet followed his path anyway. This archetype is about courage.

In their book *The Last Week*, Marcus Borg and John Dominic Crossan argue that Jesus' entry into Jerusalem on the week of the Passover was a deliberate act of nonviolent political theater, a counterpoint to the governor's military procession entering Jerusalem the same day from the opposite direction. Borg and Crossan's compelling argument helps us see that Jesus was thoughtful and deliberate in his choices, though they were choices that put him in the deadly focus of the Roman Empire.

When we are faced with the Archetype of the Crucifixion, we are invited to look at the path that led Jesus to the cross as more significant for our spiritual lives than Jesus' death on the cross itself. When we encounter the Crucifixion we are invited to think about the choices that shape our lives.

We sometimes believe that having many choices and maintaining those choices is our goal in life: We desire to have many material possessions or goods, and the more goods we have, the happier our life is. Over time, as we mature and if we are living consciously, we begin to let go of some choices, and our paths narrow. Finally, when we have reached our truest identity, which is a sublime mixture of both our choices and the acceptance of given-ness in our lives, we find that our path is more or less fixed.

At first, even though we have chosen and accepted this path, the realization that we no longer have seemingly infinite or even many choices is frightening and shocking. We also come to see that our life path, though ours, may come with great costs. This is what we see with the path of Jesus. As his ministry developed he came to see that to continue would end in his death. His redeeming power for us comes from his authentic, courageous choice to stay true to his path and calling. It did not come from the tortured death itself.

Have you come to know your own path?

FOX: Bad theology can readily over-psychologize the Crucifixion. The truth is that in the Gospels, the event is placed in a cosmic context, and many mystics have understood this. Scholarship now tells us that the temple in Jesus' time had two veils, and the front veil, which was on the outside of the building, was covered in pictures of the cosmos and the universe. When the Gospels declare that the veil of the temple was rent in two when Jesus died on the cross, this is an obvious statement that the Crucifixion was a cosmic event. Furthermore, the Temple was considered the center of the universe by the Jewish people. Liturgy, ritual, and ceremony are often considered the center of the universe. It is also Jewish teaching that when there is injustice, the whole earth is off-kilter. So again, we can easily overly psychologize and overly anthropocentrize the Crucifixion, when it is really about the brokenness of the universe that happens time and again whenever injustice triumphs. The Crucifixion speaks to the suffering of all beings—not just the suffering of Jesus.

We have already seen how the event of the Crucifixion is incorporated into the Transfiguration story via explicit statements about Jesus' impending death. Additionally, the stories of the Crucifixion present the event as cosmic: Luke says the sun was eclipsed; Matthew says, "The earth quaked; the rocks were split; the tombs opened and the bodies of many holy men rose from the dead"; Mark says that "darkness was over the whole land" and "the veil of the Temple was torn in two from top to bottom" when Jesus died (Luke 23:44; Matthew 27:52-53; Mark 15:39). The Crucifixion is a cosmic teaching since the Temple stood for the beauty and order of the cosmic structure of the universe. John's Gospel develops a recurring theme of exaltation and crucifixion, glory and darkness, where the Crucifixion is part of *doxa* or glory, which as we have seen represents the Cosmic Christ. Death is real but it does not have the last word.

English mystic Julian of Norwich understood clearly the cosmic nature of the crucifixion event when she wrote: "The sky and the earth failed at the time of Christ's dying because he, too, was part of nature." And again, "All creatures of God's creation that can suffer pain suffered with him … Those who were his friends suffered pain because they loved him." Compassion is like that, according to Julian: "I saw a great oneing between Christ and us because when he was in pain we were in pain."[54]

Buddhists remind us that all beings suffer. Suffering accompanies us wherever we find being. This same truth is borne witness by the Crucifixion. Jesus suffered; he suffered to an extreme and he suffered unjustly, for he was a good person by any ethical yardstick. So we are all reminded of pain and loss, suffering and death, limits and unfairness that life often brings our way. Suffering and grief are universal experiences, and so, too, are the limits that life presents us when our goals or dreams are not fully achieved, or any time an accident or health issues or divorce come our way. Loss happens: "All is impermanent," as the Buddhists say. No one is spared the suffering that life brings our way.

The difference between people is this: How do we find meaning in the suffering? How do we respond to it without just projecting more suffering onto others? How do we, in Leonard Cohen's words, deal with both "the Holy and the Broken" and still manage to sing "Hallelujah" or Praise to Life?[55]

All these questions, archetypal and universal that they are, are raised by the image of the crucified Christ. The Christ who suffered and died in Jesus is the same Christ who suffers and dies in us. This is why the Crucifixion is so universal a story. People—including just and good people—suffer. All beings suffer. Suffering is a cosmic habit; it is built into everything the cosmos does. Even planets and galaxies and supernovas, we now know, live, die, and resurrect by seeding other new birthings in the universe. We will address the resurrection dimension in Stations 13 and 14.

Evil seems to have a cosmological dimension to it—it is bigger than we are, it keeps recurring, it is never completely stamped out, it is smart and crafty and often has its way, it is powerful and likes to hang out with people and institutions of power. This is why evil is often attributed to the dark angelic hosts, what St. Paul calls the "powers and principalities" with whom we struggle (Ephesians 6:12). At Jesus' crucifixion these powers seemed to triumph. The Roman Empire had its way with this troublemaker and pseudo-king who preached an alternative Kingdom to that of the Empire, and who therefore had to die the ignominious death of crucifixion that the Empire doled out to the lowest of the low.

In that sense Jesus' death is an archetypal event for all those who are powerless and vulnerable to evil and power for power's sake; to imperialism that is thoroughly impersonal, uncaring, and without compassion, based only on the lust for control. At the Crucifixion these powers appeared to triumph over Jesus and all those "least" whom he called people to serve in Matthew 25—the poor and hungry, the sick and imprisoned. One can connect the Crucifixion to the Good Shepherd icon, since a good shepherd lays down his life, if necessary, for his or her flock. "No greater love does a person have than to lay down their life for their friends" (John 15:13).

But the Crucifixion is not the last word by any means in the Jesus story, or the Cosmic Christ story.

WALKING STATION 12. The Crucifixion reminds us of the universality of suffering. All beings suffer, including the Christ in Jesus and in all living things. How are we dealing with suffering in our lives? Can we face it and not run from it? Can we talk to it and ask it what it has to teach us, or why it has come back? Is there a community of sorrow and of grief that we can join and learn from and move on from? Can suffering truly open our hearts to make us large again? As Joanna Macy puts it: "When your heart breaks the whole universe can flow through."

> "O Spirit, open and stretch our hearts. Let suffering deepen and widen our souls, our consciousness, the way we understand the world and one another. Teach us what we have to learn from the Dark Night and from suffering. Lead us into circles of people where we can teach one another what grieving means, how it can deepen and refresh us, how it can make us more beautiful beings who serve one another and try to lessen what suffering we can."

13. The Resurrection

ULLRRICH JAVIER LEMUS: Resurrection for me signifies that after Jesus died, he went back with his Father, flying up to the sky, to the Infinite, with a peaceful look on his face. For this reason in my icon he is happy with his labor here, with the work that he has accomplished, and will be from now to eternity. He is in a shape of flying up as part human, part spirit, with an infinite heart and with this crown which is almost shaped like a flying saucer. We may not be the only beings in the universe. At first he wore the crown of thorns but now his crown is more glorious (*glorioso* in Spanish). He goes back to his Father very proud and very happy to have given us the blessing of his life, and to have given his meditation and his spirituality and his suffering and his pain for us. The blue color represents going up to the sky.

He is radiant. The gold color speaks to the splendor of Divinity. The crown in this case is a glorious crown, because when he died he changed the crown of thorns to a glorious crown because he was going up with the Trinity again. Also, there is the suggestion of a spaceship, because we don't know how many other beings throughout the entire universe also glorify him, how many in all the different places he's been around the universe. We are so limited here. We only have a little tiny piece of human history in our grasp, and even that is highly limited. So this event of the Resurrection is bigger than us, bigger than our anthropocentrism and everything else.

FOX: Much in the Resurrection story is set in the context of the Cosmic Christ. Those people who claimed to have encountered Jesus after he died did not claim to have seen "the historical Jesus" but "the risen Lord," in other words, the Cosmic Christ. A cosmological victory over the pessimism of death and destruction is announced by the Resurrection events. Angels are part of the stories and, as we have seen, they are part of the Cosmic Christ events from the Nativity to the glory of the first Easter Sunday. In Matthew's Gospel, an earthquake accompanies the Resurrection and an "angel of the Lord" rolls back the stone from the tomb in which Jesus was interred (Matthew 28:2).

As theologian Edward Schillebeeckx said, "In antiquity, anthropology and ethics are seen against a cosmic background, in other words, one determined by heavenly spirits. Therefore Jesus' resurrection is *ipso facto* an enthronement of the Lord Jesus over all angelic powers."[56]

The resurrection answers an age-old fear of the human species, one that psychologist Otto Rank calls the number one issue for humans, an issue that dictated the building of the pyramids and the construction of empires and the ancient cries of "God save the King." It is the fear of death and the issue of immortality. Do we survive after this life or not? Is all we do for naught? Is there an afterlife? Or do we have to build empires and pyramids to somehow ensure our immortality? The Egyptians believed that by burying the Pharaoh just right, the rest of the community could participate vicariously in his afterlife, thus, the great project of the pyramids. Otto Rank said that Jesus and Paul's teachings about resurrection "democratized immortality," and meant we were all now eligible for life after death. Resurrection is not just for kings and pharaohs, but for everyone.

This means, above all else, that we can get on with living now, because even the simplest among us need no longer fear death or take on grand projects to stave off our mortality by way of a participation mystique. That release of fear, Rank felt, was the deeper meaning of the Resurrection—and that is why he called the Resurrection "the most revolutionary idea" humans have ever come up with. (Incidentally, Rank was a Jew and not a Christian.) To believe in resurrection is to surrender our fear of death and the power that fear holds over us. It follows that one becomes critical of "immortality projects," and instead "lives in order to live," as Meister Eckhart teaches. One enters eternal life in this life instead of waiting for another.

This is why theologian Thomas Aquinas taught that there are "two resurrections." The first is waking up in this lifetime, and if you do that, you do not have to worry about the second resurrection.[57]

How much a part of Resurrection are we? How unafraid of death? How willing are we to live fully and love fully, and to act creatively? A full life is a creative life. Courageous life does not allow fear to take over; it does not submit to living vicariously. Never have the words "I have come that you may have life and have it in abundance" (John 10:10) meant so much. Life in abundance is a life fully lived.

What does the Resurrection mean to me and to my community? Have we moved beyond our fear of death—and fear of life? How does the reality of resurrection affect the ways and manners of our lives?

BISHOP MARC: What is the new life that God is seeking to give you? Has that news been obscured by dreams or patterns of thinking and acting that are no longer relevant or productive—thus "dead"—in your life?

New Testament scholars make a distinction between a resuscitation and a resurrection. When someone is resuscitated, they more or less pick up with the life they were living before the near-death event: perhaps wiser, or traumatized, but still the same person. This is not the case with a resurrection, however.

We can begin to understand something about the nature of resurrection when we look at the stories of Jesus' resurrection. We learn that his wounds were still on him, but he lived, and his mode of life now included the ability to appear and disappear and to enter locked rooms. Yet he still ate and drank as all humans do; in other words, he was not a phantasm.

You could say that as spectacular as Jesus' new powers were, they were somewhat surface when we are considering the essence of an individual's personhood. Did Jesus' core commitments and message change in the resurrection?

We could say that Jesus intensified his message, concentrating on the cosmic quality of forgiveness, making it the heart of his message. Such intensification is in continuity with what came before, however.

The new note in Jesus' post-resurrection message is the emphasis on the Spirit-formed community. "Very truly, I tell you, the one who believes in me will also do the works that I do and, in fact, will do greater works than these, because I am going to the Father," the resurrected Jesus says in John's Gospel (John 14:12). The reasons he says that you will do greater things are that first, you will do them as part of a deeply interrelated faith community, and beyond that, you will be empowered by the Spirit of God.

The work of the Resurrected Christ was always bringing others back from their own forms of death. How are you an agent of resurrection for others in your community, in your life-world?

WALKING STATION 13. The Resurrection is happening daily and cosmically. All beings—even stars and supernovas and galaxies—live, die, and resurrect. Am I aware of my many deaths and resurrections? Am I grateful for what I have learned from them? How can I assist others in their journeys through death into resurrection? How do I manifest a spirit of resurrection and joy which nothing—not even death itself—can threaten or diminish or wipe out?

> "O Spirit, make me a being who has tasted resurrection and is grateful for it. Make me one who sees the Joy in life even through the pain of suffering and loss. Make me one who truly believes in resurrection and who joins all the resurrected ones, those who have moved from death to new life."

14. "I Am the Resurrection and the Life."

M.C. RICHARDS:

I Am Dying
... I do not feel betrayed or bereft,
it's more like the Chattanooga Choo Choo:
the great traffic of evolution
and I am carrying my bit of being
free of agenda—
open to a future
Ready to experiment, be creative, serve
be beautiful, be real,
be nowhere
be no one I already know
be birthing myself
waves and particles
backpacking in the hereafter.[58]

BISHOP MARC: Martha, one of Jesus' closest friends and followers, says the following to Jesus near the cave tomb where her brother Lazarus has been buried: "Yes, Lord, I believe that you are the one who is coming into this world (the Cosmos)" (John 11:27). What we shall see is that Jesus speaks in this story as the representative of the cosmos, and of the divine power that animates the cosmos. The "I Am" saying in this story, "I am Resurrection and Life," is truly a Cosmic Christ station: Christ met as a cosmic force and being.

What is the import; what is at issue in this story—the Raising of Lazarus from the dead? Put another way, why is the Christ showing up; for what purpose? Both the setting—the tomb of Lazarus who has just died four days before—and the words spoken by Martha when Jesus arrives at the tomb—"If you had been here my brother would not have died" (John 11:21)—establish that death is the great theme with which we are struggling.

Because Jesus is acclaimed by Mary as a cosmic being, the theme of death is equally all-encompassing: not just the death of our bodies, but the deaths of species and cultures, the deaths of stars and galaxies. There are also the deaths we experience in the midst of life—failures, isolation, rejection, injustices, and especially imprisonment, where we are shut off from the everyday world of friendship, love, and community.

Lazarus has died, and his body has been put in a cave tomb, so we notice that while Lazarus has disappeared from our sight, Jesus is "the one who is coming into the world." The meaning of death is, in part, about being concealed, cut off from the sight of others. When someone says, "He/she is dead to me," they intend the meaning that one layer of this story uses: that of death within society. Mortal death, the death of the body, is a continuation of death-within-life.

All these deaths, from the scale of the cosmos to the injustices experienced all the way down to the slights we feel, are of one piece. When a star dies, though, we can see that this death produces new, varied, abundant life. Elements are thrown out from the death pangs of the star, and life reemerges in new forms. The death of a star is unbelievably violent, yet we do not view this death as bad or negative. We take a long view of the death of a star, seeing the star "living on" in the varied life that derives from it after it is extinguished. If we could stand "above" our own lives, and see the subtle and varied lines of life that extend beyond us in space and time, and that are nourished and strengthened, sheltered and birthed from our lives, how would this affect our fear of death?

Joe Henderson, a famous Jungian analyst of the last century, held that we fear the unknown within death. But is a fear of the unknown so widespread? Don't we have many people in our culture who relish the exploration of the unknown, and don't we admire these people? Even if we feel timid ourselves about the unknown, we feel we ought to embrace it.

Further, we are accumulating more and more accounts of near-death experiences, credible reports of what people have seen and felt at the moment of what might well have been their death. There is a remarkable similarity between many near-death accounts, and the experience is overwhelmingly positive. Despite our zest for the unknown and the witness of many who attest that life after death is a state of beatitude, death is feared by most people.

Jesus' own story may help us understand another aspect of the fear of death. Shortly after Lazarus is raised from the dead, the Gospel tells us that a plot among government authorities was hatched to kill Lazarus, because he was a living certification of Jesus' extraordinary powers. And within a very short while after that plot, Jesus himself is executed in a gruesome, extended, painful, and humiliating way. In cultures marked by violence, where death is employed as a means of control, the spread of fear is deliberate and is transferred to death with its nimbus of the unknown. Then death is no longer alluring but terrifying. The fear of death is spread ever further.

In our own time, we have sequestered old age, illness, and most of all death away from day-to-day life, as if these states of being are somehow not ordinary. This hiddenness makes death frightening. We might say that the paralysis that is felt around death—a paralysis that is the result of great fear—is itself a kind of death-in-life.

It is this death-in-life that Jesus confronts in the story of the raising of Lazarus. Martha speaks of resurrection as a future event, something that signals the end of time, perhaps in the far distant future. Jesus responds with an affirmation of relationship in the present: "I Am the Resurrection and the Life."

Jesus did not mean that he was the only one to ever bear the cosmic message of new life. Rather, he is saying that in our one-to-one relationships, patterned by love, we find courage for living, for throwing off paralysis and the fear of death—and in doing so, we are therefore resurrected. Each of us can be bearers of that message for others.

Like Jesus, you bear astounding cosmic powers of Life and Resurrection. Remember that the Christ is saying that he is both the general resurrection awaited by the faithful, and that he is the life principle itself. As we accept our place in the cosmos, we more and more understand that these cosmological powers reside in us, as well as in him, and in great cosmic entities like galaxies. The Cosmic Christ dwells everywhere and in all of us.

If this power within you is hard to believe, listen to Jesus asking Martha this question about the power of Resurrection and Life: "Do you believe this?" Let this question resonate within you and listen quietly to what emerges.

FOX: Who does not seek Resurrection? Who does not seek a full and fuller life? Did Jesus not promise, "I have come that you may have life, life in abundance?" (John 10:10)

> How am I Resurrection for others?
> How am I Life for others?

To be Resurrection for another I need to be Resurrection for myself. That means I cannot dwell in darkness and death and anger and oppression and submission and resentment and pain forever. I need to wake up, get up, rise up, put on life even when days are dark and my soul is down and shadows surround me everywhere. I have to refuse to participate in my own oppression. I need to learn forgiveness, let go, and move on. I must give birth: I must create, put myself out there, be a mother, be a carrier of new life. I have to listen to the voice that says:

"Be resurrection."

"Break out of your tombs; do not settle for death. Break out. Stand up. Give birth. Get out of easy pessimism and lazy cynicism. Put your heart and mind and hands to creating hope and light and resurrection. Be born again. And again. And again. Rise up and be counted. Rise up and imbibe the good news deeply—that death does not conquer, that life, not death, has the last word, that all things change form but also get reborn or resurrected."

"I am the Resurrection." So are you and so is everyone else. Resurrection is a commitment to hope and being reborn. It is a commitment to creativity, to the Spirit who "makes all things new" (Revelation 21:5). Resurrection is the Spirit's work. It is life of the Spirit.

And what about Life? How am I Life? How living and alive am I? How much in love with life am I? Can anyone or any event separate me from my love of life? Paul the mystic asks (and then answers), "Who shall separate us from the love of God? Neither death nor life, height nor depth, neither present nor future" (Romans 8:35, 38). Is my curiosity alive? My gratitude? My mind? My imagination? My laughter and sense of humor? My creativity? My powers of generosity and compassion? My powers for continually generating and regenerating life?

Many mystics—from Hildegard of Bingen to Thomas Aquinas to Meister Eckhart to Howard Thurman—say, "God is life." Thus to say, "I am fully alive and fully in love with life" means that I am feeling fully the God presence in me—I am in love with God who is Life; the living God. And to say "I am the Life" is to say "I am God," or at least a part of God, a son or daughter of God, an expression, an offspring, a manifestation, an incarnation of God. Another Christ.

How are we doing? Are we growing in God-like-ness? In God action? In works of justice and compassion and healing and celebrating? To celebrate life is to celebrate God, to thank God for life, to worship. How are we doing in expressing the "sheer joy" of God (Aquinas) as well as the justice of God?

Yes, I am, yes, we are, the Resurrection and the Life. We bring aliveness and rebirth and plenty of hope into the world, however dark the news becomes. That is what it means to believe in Easter Sunday and the Resurrection. We become Resurrection and the Life. Christ rises anew.

WALKING STATION 14. Am I resurrection for others? How am I that aspect of the Cosmic Christ? How might I become the resurrected Christ more fully? Am I life for others? How so? How can I bring more of my life-giving qualities to the world?

"O Spirit, teach me the truths of resurrection and resurrecting, and the deepest truths of Life itself, now, in this life. How many times have I died? And how many times have I resurrected? Or refused to resurrect? Grant me the courage to let go, and the trust to forgive, move on, and to live life fully, even when death in any of its forms assaults me."

15. Ascension

ULLRRICH JAVIER LEMUS: The Ascension represents Christ going up to the heavens or into the infinite universe, in the form of a green man with one hand reaching up and one leaving the material earth of the material body. The shape is—in my interpretation—an animal, a dragon. It's a dragon leaf, and it's green because he's just leaving earth. And the purple represents Christ's pain due to suffering here on earth. Purple also represents spirituality. Christ is reaching up, leaving this earth with pain because he loves us. But he is also leaving his legacy, and the figures of labyrinth or infinite circles speak of the universe where he is going.

Regarding the dragon, I once had a magnificent dream about a white dragon looking at me with big blue eyes, and shimmering scales, and he was beautiful. I never forgot that dream and what it represented. This shimmering white beautiful dragon was, to me, God, in my dream. It was fierce, and powerful, and big. It was wide, and that got into my mind. I tried to put it here as it resides in my consciousness. Now it is emerging. Then I put two and two together and I realized, "Oh, that's the dream that I had!" So then I put it here, you know. I never forget that dream—it's the most powerful and transcendent dream I ever had. That's what I tried to portray here.

FOX: The following liturgical text is presented for the feast of the Ascension: "The God of glory ... has seated Christ at the right hand of divinity in heaven, high above every principality, power, virtue and domination, and every name that can be given in this age or the age to come. God has put all things under Christ's feet and has made him thus exalted, head of the church, which is his body: the fullness of the one who fills the universe in all its parts" (Ephesians 1:17-23). Notice how flooded this passage is with imagery and themes that denote the Cosmic Christ.

A second text from the Feast of the Ascension is from the Book of Acts, and it invokes images of the "sky," the "clouds," the "ends of the earth," and other signs of the Cosmic Christ. It reads: "'You will receive power when the Holy Spirit comes down on you; then you are to be my witnesses in Jerusalem, throughout Judea and Samaria, yes, even to the ends of the earth.' No sooner had he said this than he was lifted up before their eyes in a cloud which took him from their sight. They were still gazing up into the heavens when two men dressed in white stood beside them. 'People of Galilee,' they said, 'why do you stand here looking up at the skies? This Jesus who has been taken from you will return, just as you saw him go up into the heavens'" (Acts 1:8-11).

There is a subtle echo here of the events at the Baptism and the Transfiguration, when the sky opened up and a Godly voice spoke praising the Christ as a "beloved" one. But now we are the beloved, as the sky opens up and absorbs the Christ in Jesus.

The late Buckminster Fuller remarked that anyone who is still using the words "up and down" is 400 years out of date. In a curved universe there is no up and down, only in and out. Pilots do not radio to the control tower that they are "flying up and flying down" but that they are "flying in and flying out." So, too, the Ascension is not about Jesus going "up" but "out"—out to the furthest reaches of the universe. The Ascension event is reminding us that the Christ presence is felt in the furthest corners of the universe. We are not just dwellers in our little villages on this modest planet; we share in cosmic events and we carry the Cosmic Christ within us—the very "fullness of the one who fills the universe in all its parts." That is our destiny, to partake in such cosmic events. Life is neither petty nor small but grand and immense. We are made for cosmic events.

BISHOP MARC: The validation of the body and all of creation is the theme of the Ascension. This is the call to avoid abstraction in life.

It may strike you as odd when you meet the Archetype of the Ascension of Christ to learn that this rising into the Cosmos is a validation of all that is created, rather than a goodbye to it all. There are stories of the spiritual path that envision a leaving behind of this complicated, unreliable thing—the physical, our bodies, and all the world with which they are connected—but these narratives are not those of Christianity.

It was my great coauthor Matthew Fox who helped turn Western Christianity back to its ancient affirmation of all that is created, via his germinal book, *Original Blessing* (as distinct from original sin or curse). It is a slow journey back. As one of my teachers at St. Elizabeth Mental Hospital in Washington, D.C., used to say, "It takes about as long to get out of something as it took to get into it." Such a formulation is realistic, but not the last word, as it doesn't take into account forgiveness and grace.

Jesus the Christ rises into the heavens with his body and the wounds of the Crucifixion. What we may understand is that by doing so, he carries Creation back to its source. This is a reaffirmation of its original blessed state, or perhaps a healing and restoration of the Creation.

Let us press this idea a little further. In the United States, obituaries are usually pretty bland pieces of writing. This is because they are one-sided, giving only a list of the deceased's accomplishments and honors. Obituaries in the United Kingdom are different; they tell a more complete but still loving story of the person who has died.

Jesus ascending into the heavens with his wounded body is a more complete story. Part of what we carry to God is our woundedness, our failures, our hesitations and fears. One of the single most important words in the spiritual lexicon is *acceptance*.

When you come to the Archetype of the Ascension, included there is an invitation to receive the truth of your blessed, beloved status with God, complete with all that is wounded about you. Can you see yourself as God does?

WALKING STATION 15. The Ascension reminds us to move out, to expand—as the universe is always expanding. In other words, to grow. Meister Eckhart says that God is delighted to watch your soul expand in works of justice. Are we delighting God? Joy expands the soul. The joy of resurrection assists the expansion of ascension. Learning also expands us. Am I always learning? Curiosity opens the door to expansion of mind and consciousness. How precious and holy is curiosity in my life? Am I developing my muscles of curiosity, not about gossip and trivia, but about things that matter? Things such as the place of humans in the universe, and the risk the universe took in taking a chance on birthing our species?

"O Spirit, befriend the expansion of our souls, the joy that grows our souls, the learning that expands our consciousness; and our moving beyond rigid tribal boxes of religion, ethnicity, nationhood, or gender to become the fulsome and expanded people we are meant to be."

16. Pentecost

ULLRRICH JAVIER LEMUS: This clay piece is made of volcanic rock and pyrite and tourmaline, along with resin and colored tile mixed into the clay. The pure minerals tell the history of the universe, through which the Holy Spirit creates and has always created. The glass forms a kind of mirror, inviting the viewer to look inside to find the Cosmic Christ and the Holy Spirit within himself or herself. The transparency of the colored glass echoes the colored stained glass of Grace Cathedral.

This piece is very earthy, with pure clay and rocks which conjure up the fire that the Holy Spirit is so often identified with (as at Pentecost, the flames of fire). The fire is ancient and it is cosmic and burns in the center of the earth. These same elements are found everywhere in the universe, so they are cosmic elements.

The rocks are alive! I created this piece by cooking the minerals into the clay.

Thus the Holy Spirit is modern and about the "new," but it is also rustic and about the ancient goings-on in the universe. This piece is actually two pieces in one—the outer form, which is earthy and includes minerals of the earth, holds and embraces the inner piece, which is essentially rock. The earth is embracing and holding the rock much as it embraces and holds us. When the Pentecost story talks about "all the nations of the earth" gathering, it invites us to go beyond a human consciousness. Our Mother Earth is larger than human nations or tribes or religions—it is that which binds us all. All beings are beings of Mother Earth.

So I represent the rock nations and the stone nations and the winged ones in this tablet. There is an honoring of the elders as well, for rocks are the oldest beings among us. This is one reason they are welcomed to lead our prayers in a sweat lodge. The promise of Pentecost is about making all things new. A consciousness of Mother Earth mothering all beings on our planet would contribute greatly to making human history different and new, more peaceful and just.

BISHOP MARC: Pentecost is an early Christian name for a Jewish festival of the time of Jesus. The earliest Christians still worshipped as Jews and were members of synagogues. This is not unlike the Buddha Siddhartha Gautama and his earliest followers, who were reformers within the Hinduism of his time (circa 500 B.C.E.). Jews from many cultural and language groups had come to Jerusalem for the celebration of Pentecost (the Jewish festival is Shavuot) in the weeks after Jesus' execution and the stories of his resurrection from the dead. Suddenly, mystical flames appeared above the heads of a group of proto-Christians who were in Jerusalem for the festival. Others who were nearby heard the proto-Christians speak, and everyone who heard their words heard them in the listener's own language. The story of Pentecost appears in the Acts of the Apostles, a book of the New Testament (Acts 2:1-31).

The story of Pentecost comes near the end of the Christian Bible and is the reversal of the confusion and isolation and enmity in our world that the Tower of Babel, a story in the first book of the Bible, symbolizes. But how is this reversal accomplished? What restores the relatedness of the world?

At Pentecost, Jesus the Christ's promise to send the Holy Spirit to begin the constitution of a new Presence on the Earth begins its fulfillment. Now Christ is present in the world not primarily as an individual, but as a community. The work of the Holy Spirit at Pentecost is to make the "blood" of this new "body" flow; that is, to create channels of mutual communication and nourishment between individuals who beforehand were not aware of their essential interconnection.

Spirit and fire appear in the Archetype of the Pentecost. Spirit and fire are paired in the opening of the Gospel of Matthew. John the Baptist announces that he, John, performs baptism using water, and that his baptism is a rite for amendment of life, for repentance. But, John proclaims, there is a prophet coming after him who will baptize with spirit and with fire! (Matthew 3:11)

What do spirit and fire mean in Matthew, and in the Acts of the Apostles in the Pentecost story? Fire is the universal fact of suffering. Spirit is the ever-present God who stays with even the sparrow who falls, allowing the possibility that suffering can produce meaning. The fire of suffering comes to all, and yet the Spirit of God is present to all who suffer. It heals and produces understanding in suffering's wake.

Some suffering is the result of greed. Mythologist Joseph Campbell taught that the meaning of the Western dragon is the greedy ego. It hoards treasure and beautiful women, neither of which it can relate to meaningfully, but wants and must have nevertheless. In Wagner's *Ring Cycle*, when the hero Siegfried kills the dragon Fafner, he is not killing a creature outside himself but is recognizing the deathly quality of his own greed. When he tastes the blood of Fafner, he can understand the language of the birds. When greed no longer burns in me, I can awaken to the language of others, or I can "speak their language."

When you come to the Archetype of the Pentecost, you are being invited into full participation in the community of faith. What dragon of your soul must give way for this to take place?

FOX: Pentecost is a feast day steeped in cosmic imagery. All four elements—the physics of the day—played a role: *wind (air)* came into the room where the fearful disciples gathered; tongues of *fire* descended on the disciples; *water* accompanied the many baptisms; all nations of the *earth* gathered. Just as the Tower of Babel story tells of the cosmic chaos that overtakes the human race and creates separation, so the various peoples of the Earth that heard the events at Pentecost in their own language tell of a healing of the divisions of the people of the Earth. Creation and its order triumphs over chaos and disorder. Babbling comes to an end; understanding reigns. Listen to the many cosmic elements in the telling of the story in Acts:

> Suddenly they heard what sounded like a powerful wind from heaven, the noise of which filled the entire house in which they were sitting; and something appeared to them that seemed like tongues of fire; these separated and came to rest on the head of each of them. They were all filled with the Holy Spirit and began to speak foreign languages as the Spirit gave them the gift of speech. Now there were devout people living in Jerusalem from every nation under heaven, and at this sound they all assembled, everyone bewildered to hear these people speaking in their own language.
>
> —Acts 2:2-6

Peter's sermon to the assembled peoples is taken from the prophet Joel, and it, too, is filled with cosmic imagery and meaning. Invoking Joel, Peter preaches the following:

> In the days to come—it is the Lord who speaks—
> I will pour out my spirit on all humankind
> Their sons and daughters shall prophesy,
> your young people shall see visions,
> your old people shall dream dreams ...
> I will display portents in heaven above
> and signs on earth below.
> The sun will be turned into darkness and the moon into blood
> before the great Day of the Lord dawns.
> All who call on the name of the Lord will be saved.
>
> —Acts 2:17-21

This story celebrates the Spirit bringing about intergenerational wisdom and sharing. How are we doing today in this regard? Are the young people seeing visions and are the elders supporting these visions? Are the old ones dreaming dreams and sharing them with the young? Are elders responding to their vocation as elders, and in turn are they interacting with the youth? And what are the visions and dreams about? Are they just about giving birth to more gadgets and distractions? Or are they about new and deeper relationships with our ancestors and the Earth and her creatures? About healing our inner selves, so that peace can finally come to the earth, so that our right brains might flourish and our mammal-compassionate brains might emerge more fully than our aggressive and reptilian brains?

Peter concludes his talk with an appeal to the Cosmic Christ when he says: "The whole House of Israel can be certain that God has made this Jesus whom you crucified both Lord and Christ" (Acts 2:36).

Clearly the event of Pentecost, which tradition likes to link with the birth of the church, is a cosmic moment and a telling of a cosmic story about the Cosmic Christ. The Epistle for the day is from Romans 8 and is about how all of creation groans and hopes for healing. The Spirit who comes is the creative Spirit that birthed all of creation. It is unrestricted. It blows where it will. All are recipients.

In John's Gospel, the Pentecost event is presented as the risen Christ breathing the breath of life into the disciples (just as God breathed life into the original Adam) and extending peace unto them. Bishop John Shelby Spong equates this event with "the second coming," and tells us, "The second coming is the birth of all those who choose the light and enter into the mystical source of oneness with God … It was the new creation. To be born of the spirit was to be born into the meaning and oneness of God … It was to enter in a new way what it means to be human."[59]

WALKING STATION 16. The Pentecost event promises us that the spirit will be poured out "on all humankind," and that the young and old will be alive with intergenerational wisdom and creativity, birthing new ways of relating and communicating. How are we doing? Isn't our Babel-like world—currently so often divided by religion and nation and race and gender and gender preference—interfering with this promise? How can my calling and vocation bridge the divisions among humans, and between humans and other species, thus bringing unity anew?

> "O Spirit, make of me a person endowed with a Spirit that heals divisions and brings tribes together instead of keeping them apart. Endow me with a Spirit that unites Father Sky and Mother Earth into a Sacred Marriage, one that embodies a balance of Compassion and of Justice, action and contemplation, becoming and being."

PART TWO
FURTHER
PRACTICES FOR
CONNECTING TO
THE DIVINE

1. ADDITIONAL "I AM" STATEMENTS

In addition to the classic seven "I Am" statements that the authors and the artists feature in this book, others exist as well. We list them here, along with accompanying meditations.

I. "I Am He, the one who is speaking to you."—John 4:26

This is the most important of the "I Am" statements, never listed in the primary set of "I Ams," which unlike this statement are metaphoric. This "I Am" is the expression of a fully realized person. The exploration of all the other "I Am" statements is the path toward this integrated, courageous declaration of oneself.

The great "I Am" statements that have played such an important role in shaping the spiritual life of Christianity are generally held to be seven in number. Their selection from among the many "I Am" statements in the Gospel of John was an early choice within emerging Christianity, one which has been accepted and used for many centuries.

Now we are in a position to see that these seven great "I Am" statements are held between two "I Am" declarations (these are iterations of the same statement, emphasizing their importance). All together, the seven metaphoric "I Am" statements and their framing "I Am" declarations represent a metaphoric system. These seven great "I Am" statements are all meant to cast light forward and backward on the two statements that contain them.

What are these two containing "I Am" statements, for which the seven "I Ams" are needed for understanding and interpretation? They are as humble and as magnificent as is possible in our life: the declaration of Jesus' authentic being—I Am he, Jesus of Nazareth, the Messiah. Humble because "I Am he" points to the earthly person of Jesus; magnificent because "I Am" is the transcendent Name of God given in the Book of Exodus to the Prophet Moses.

The first of these foundational statements comes near the beginning of the Gospel of John. Jesus has met a Samaritan woman at Jacob's well. Their teasing, mysterious dialogue is under way, and she says, "I know that the Messiah is coming, who, when he comes will proclaim all things to us." Jesus answers, "I Am he, the one who is speaking to you" (John 4:26).

After this great dialogue, we begin to encounter the metaphoric "I Am" statements we have considered in Part One above: I Am the Light; I Am the Living Bread; I Am the Vine; I Am the Good Shepherd; I Am the Door; I Am the Way, the Truth and the Life; I Am the Resurrection and the Life. Our consciousness of this human being who declared himself to the woman at the well deepens with each metaphoric "I Am."

II. "I Am He."—John 18:5

Then we come to the climactic end of John's Gospel. Jesus has washed his disciples' feet and they are in the midst of what will be their last meal together before Jesus' death. Judas receives bread from Jesus, and then leaves the table and the room where they are eating. The narrator writes, at this point, the simple and devastating statement, "And it was night." Here is the point at which the Light is most imperiled, the Shadow most dilated and threatening.

Jesus teaches his disciples one last time, and prays for them. Then he leads them all into the night, into a garden. Judas meets them with a group of Temple police and Roman soldiers.

> Then Jesus, knowing all that was to happen to him, came forward and asked them, "For whom are you looking?" They answered, "Jesus of Nazareth." Jesus replied, "I am he." Judas, who betrayed him, was standing with them. When Jesus said to them, "I am he," they stepped back and fell to the ground.
>
> —John 18:4-5

It is easy to miss the extraordinary happening that occurred when Jesus made the simple declaration, "I Am he." We are told that a contingent of police and soldiers fell to the ground before him. We are in the position of that crowd around Jesus in the night garden. We have slowly prayed our way from the first puzzling, impossible declaration, "I Am he, the one who is speaking to you," through all the great metaphoric "I Am" statements, and now we hear the divine name spoken not from within a burning bush but from a human being.

When you stand before the Archetype "I Am he, Jesus of Nazareth," you are standing before a holy mirror. Jesus desired not worshippers, but followers. To what extent can you claim both your full humanity and the indwelling Spirit of God?

III. "I Am the Alpha and the Omega."—Revelation 22:13

There is a spiral structure to our life's path. The Cosmic Christ speaks these words, "I Am the Alpha and the Omega, the Beginning and the End," in the book that concludes the Bible, the Apocalypse of John. The Apocalypse of John or Book of Revelation was produced by the same community that brought forth the Gospel of John and the Letters of John, and these sacred texts share continuity of symbol usage throughout.

At the opening of the Gospel of John, we learn that the Logos, which is the Cosmic Christ as the creative patterning energy of God, was present from the beginning of the universe, and helped bring the universe into being (see Station 1 above). Now, in the Apocalypse, the Logos speaks as the One who brings all things to their completion and restores the universe's essential unity.

Sacred time has been presented as a complete, perfect circle, with the Cosmic Christ present both at the beginning of all that is and also awaiting the future to bring all to fulfillment.

Nineteenth-century romantics and esotericists deepened our view of time and history by saying that we are on a spiral path. We return to the point of origin, but on another plane, enriched by the journey.

The spiral structure of reality allows for breakthroughs. The universe is not a closed system; there is truth that goes beyond the conservation of energy. Love breaks into even the bleakest situation and transforms everything.

Thus, when we meet Christ as the Alpha and the Omega, it is the present, not the past or the distant future that is the matter for our meditation and prayer. Do you experience some part of your life as enclosed in a perfect circle, with no real change possible? This is the moment to pray for a breakthrough, the in-breaking of love into what felt like a closed system.

Or, could you be that miracle for someone you know? Who in your life-world seems to exist in a closed circle? Remember that the true miracle is not to seek to solve the problem internal to the circle for someone else, but rather to open the system to surprise, the new, the loving.

This "I Am" statement of the Cosmic Christ comes at the very end of the Christian Bible. With this statement the great drama of the Bible, from its cosmic beginning to its apocalyptic end, closes, and it does so on a note of healing and renewal. "I Am the Alpha and the Omega" is about God's universal powers bathing our world, restoring harmony and true life.

At the end of the Book of Revelation, when the Cosmic Christ utters the concluding "I Am statement "I Am the Alpha and the Omega, the Beginning and the End," two elements that signal discord, separation, and suffering are reintroduced. These elements are the Tree of Life and the City, both of which first appeared in the beginning of the great Bible story.

When God banishes the first humans from the walled garden of peace and plenty, it is because of their overweening desire for immortality. The symbol of this desire is the Tree of Life, one of two extraordinary trees planted at the center of the garden (the other being the Tree of the Knowledge of Good and Evil). After the first humans have eaten from the Tree of the Knowledge of Good and Evil, God sees the boundless wanting in humans and separates them from the Tree of Immortality before they eat of that sacred tree too.

In the spiritual story of human beginnings, in the next generation there is the account of a jealous young man who murders his brother. The young man Cain's parents were those banished from the garden. Now, in the next generation, humanity moves into greater separation and isolation: God banishes Cain from the community of his family. Immediately upon hearing God pronounce his exile, Cain builds the first city. Thus, the city is a symbol of our separateness from God, the Earth, and each other.

The city is also closely associated with the human drive for power and possessions. The great epic of Joseph, also found in the first book of the Bible (Genesis), illustrates the ambivalent meaning of cities. While in the pharaoh's jail (another product of the urban world), Joseph is called upon to interpret the pharaoh's disturbing dreams.

The pharaoh has two dreams that Joseph interprets as the foretelling of an intense drought-induced famine. Joseph advises the pharaoh to store grain for seven years, and then dole the grain out over the seven years of drought. This plan will save lives, yet it also represents a tremendous concentration of power. Cities are both the foundation of society and culture, yet they also abet tyranny and despotism.

After a dizzying narrative spanning a millennium of history, and with roots in the origin of the universe itself, the Bible story reaches its conclusion in the Book of Revelation (the Apocalypse). In the Revelator's vision, it is only after a series of cataclysms that a final scene of beatitude is described. Now the Tree of Life reappears, and its leaves are freely offered for "the healing of the nations" (Revelation 22:2). Likewise, the Heavenly City descends and is placed in the midst of the garden, a marrying of symbols that had previously been opposed to one another.

The Tree of Life is available to all for the purpose of healing; the City is purified and made holy and is set in the midst of the garden. What could have worked such a sharp change, from broken to healed and whole? Christian theology has largely answered the question of the healing of the Cosmos as being the work of Jesus in his self-sacrifice on the cross. In fact Jesus' death on the cross was only a part of the sacrifice; his saving work goes on beyond his death.

Let us look just a little at these ideas. First, sacrifice is a cosmic idea, as it transcends human being and experience. In their classic book *The Universe Story*, Thomas Berry and Brian Swimme write lyrically about the self-sacrifice of stars, particularly the star named Tiamat, whose supernova explosion gave birth to our solar system. "Some five billion years after the beginning of time, the star Tiamat emerged in our spiral galaxy. Tiamat knit together wonders in its fiery belly, and then sacrificed itself, carving its body up in a supernova explosion that dispersed this new elemental power in all directions, so that the adventure might deepen."[60] Drawing a parallel between cosmic creation and that of the human world, it would be safe to say that the greatest creative efforts have been made by people willing to make sacrifices.

The idea of sacrifice, and particularly the sacrifice of Jesus' life, needs to be expanded beyond his last hours of torture and execution. Sacrifice is itself a broader idea than blood sacrifice. We may understand it to be a concentrated focus on a goal to the exclusion of all other choices—those other choices are released from one's expectations; they are sacrificed. Jesus, in fact, clung to his goal of working for the liberation and healing of the world so tenaciously that even the sacrifice of his mortal life was not something he rejected.

U.K. Old Testament scholar Margaret Barker has made a powerful and sustained argument that Jesus saw himself as the successor to and the pinnacle of a great line of people who had devoted themselves to restoring the unity of the world, and that he was acknowledged in this way by his disciples as well. Jesus sacrificed his life for the goal of restoring cosmic unity.[61] His sacrifice was the sacrifice of his life: a living sacrifice. He foresaw his death as the predictable result of a mission that would put him at odds with the Roman Empire, and he continued to choose this costly path.

Part of an early Christian hymn embedded by St. Paul in one of his letters crystalizes the concept of a living sacrifice:

Let the same mind be in you that was in Christ Jesus,
who, though he was in the
form of God
did not regard equality with God
as something to be exploited, but emptied himself,
taking the form of a slave,
being born in human likeness. And being found in human form,
he humbled himself
and became obedient to the point of death—even death on a cross.
Therefore God also highly exalted him and gave him the name
that is above every name.

—Philippians 2:5-9

What is noteworthy is that the emptying (the sacrifice of choices) is prior to Jesus' death, and the death is a consequence of the sacrifice in life. Matthew Fox has helped us understand this most important distinction between the saving work of Jesus' life and the overemphasis on Jesus' death in Western Christian spirituality. It is Dr. Fox's designation of Cosmic Christ events that opens the door to seeing the true significance of Jesus' sacrifice.

The work of Jesus in restoring cosmic unity did not end with his death. In fact, the ultimate quality of his sacrifice means that he became One who prays for us all throughout time. As Paul's letter to the Romans says, "It is Christ Jesus, who dies, yes, who was raised, who is at the right hand of God, who indeed intercedes for us" (Romans 8:34). Jesus is now, as a result of the purity and concentration of his sacrifice, one who prays for us at all times, advancing the work of restoring harmony and the integrity of creation.

Finally, the work of cosmic healing is handed over in part by the Christ to all those who see and value this goal and decide to make a similar sacrifice of their own lives. The expansion of the life sacrifice of Jesus to those who follow him is what leads the Christ in the Gospel of John to make the extraordinary prediction, "Greater things will you do than I have done, because I am going to the Father" (John 14:12).

When you meditate on this Cosmic Christ saying, "I Am the Alpha and the Omega," it might be a good moment to bring to mind all those who have willingly sacrificed to forward your life. You might also ask what you have yourself sacrificed. How did Jesus come to make such a focused, extraordinary sacrifice? What does this "I Am" saying prompt in your own heart and mind?

IV. "You say that I Am a king."—John 18:37

This is the oddest of all the "I Am" statements; a kind of anti-"I Am" statement. The setting is near the end of the story of Jesus' life. He has been hauled in front of the imperial governor Pilate, who says he's heard that Jesus is the king of the Jews. Rather than affirming or denying this, Jesus answers somewhat enigmatically: "You say that I Am a king." Why does Jesus do this?

If the force of the gospel narrative were not so clear we might suppose that Jesus is making a last-minute attempt to save his life. By not claiming something that would immediately condemn him as a rebel against Rome, or denying the same thing when a myriad of accusers had already made the charge against him, there might be some slim chance of surviving this interrogation. But the four gospels are univocal in showing Jesus as having predicted his death.

So perhaps the archetype of king doesn't fit Jesus as a leader. The gospels identify Jesus as the descendant of Israel's most famous king, David. David, however, is a paradoxical king—a shepherd boy, not raised in the court, and the youngest, not the impressive oldest brother.[62] The man who anoints the young shepherd to be king is a spiritual marvel—a prophet, judge, and wonder-worker named Samuel. Samuel represents the end of the age when Israel was ruled not by kings (as the surrounding nations were) but by judges, and Samuel, on behalf of God, resists adopting the institution of kingship for Israel. When the elders of Israel petition Samuel for a king, he responds:

These will be the ways of the king who will reign over you: he will take your sons and appoint them to his chariots and to be his horsemen, and to run before his Chariots … He will take your daughters to be perfumers and cooks and bakers. He will take the best of your fields and vineyards and olive orchards and give them to his courtiers. He will take one-tenth of your grain and of your vineyards and give it to his officers and courtiers. He will take … the best of your cattle and donkeys, and put them to his work. You shall be his slaves. In that day you will cry out because of your king, whom you have chosen for yourselves; but the Lord will not answer you in that day.

—1 Samuel 8:11-18

The Old Testament presents kingship as another declension from intimacy with God. The whole period of the judges and the subsequent period of kings in Israel follows 400 years of slavery in Egypt under a king. In the dialogue between Pilate and Jesus from the New Testament, Jesus deflects the archetype of king, even though the New Testament gospels also use king-related imagery. However, alternative images are also present, as we will shortly discuss.

In the Gospel of Luke there is a subtle use of kingly imagery in the story of Jesus' birth. On the night of Jesus' birth there are shepherds guarding their flocks some distance outside the town of Bethlehem, where the story says Jesus was born.

As the shepherds go about their routine work, they see an appearance of a great crowd of angels, one of whom tells them of Jesus' birth in these words:

Do not be afraid. I bring you good news that will cause great joy for all the people. Today in the town of David a Savior has been born to you; he is the Messiah, the Lord. This will be a sign to you: You will find a baby wrapped in cloths and lying in a manger.

—Luke 2:11-12

In the Greek description of this company of angels, they are seen as a soldier army. The existence of an angelic army implies a king. Perhaps that king is the newborn child, or perhaps is God—the text is unclear. But the story goes on to say that Mary, Jesus' mother, received all this news—the Messiah status of her son; the presence of the angelic army; the designation of Jesus as Savior—and took it into her inner self. There, in her heart, the gospel says she let the ideas clash with one another.[63] Part of what is discordant concerns this military imagery associated with God. Some light is shed on this insofar as the title "Savior" was also utilized at that time as a title for the Roman emperor.

We finally see the purpose of the angelic army in the last book of the Christian Bible, the Book of the Apocalypse. In this book the angelic army, led by the archangel Michael, wars with a diabolical army (Revelation 12:7). The diabolical ones are cast out of heaven. "Diabolical" is a precise word to describe what evil does to God's cosmos—it means to break the integrity of the cosmos. Thus, the way the angelic army fights the demons must not be by violence—which is a simple continuation by replacement of one diabolical force for another—but by an entirely different use of energy: the energy of love. Love binds up and restores the original unity of the universe. Love is the weapon of the angels.

The Bible challenges monolithic king-related metaphors by complicating them, as in "shepherd-king." At times the Bible also gives us a striking alternative to language about kings, power, and violence. A truly beautiful example comes in both the gospels of Luke and Matthew. Luke's Gospel offers alternative imagery:

> At that very hour some Pharisees came and said to him, "Get away from here, for Herod wants to kill you." He said to them, "Go and tell that fox for me, 'Listen, I am casting out demons and performing cures today and tomorrow, and on the third day I finish my work. Yet today, tomorrow, and the next day I must be on my way, because it is impossible for a prophet to be killed away from Jerusalem.' Jerusalem, Jerusalem, the city that kills the prophets and stones those who are sent

desired to gather your children together as a hen gathers her brood under her wings, and you were not willing!"

—Luke 13:31-34

In this extraordinary passage Jesus calls Herod the king a fox and compares the frightened Jewish people, who are in danger of being scattered, to chicks. He himself, the Christ, is a mother hen who hopes to gather the scattered people back together into a unity under sheltering wings. This is a very Jesus metaphor—startling and jarring!

When we are confronted by this statement of the Cosmic Christ, "You say that I Am a King," this is a rare opportunity to step back and look at the remarkable pervasiveness of power-based, patriarchal, hierarchically-oriented language that shapes our sense of reality. I was honored some time ago to serve for six years on the Episcopal Church's Committee on the Status of Women. We set an operating procedure for our meetings: When we put notes on whiteboard or newsprint, we didn't call the different items "bullet points," instead calling them just "points." Since then colleagues of mine have started calling them "peace points!" The practice makes many people smile and laugh, and also gives us an opening to think about the language usage that abounds around power and violence. To ask yourself questions about language, to be jarring and startling like Jesus was in his use of metaphors—this is the ministry of angels.

V. "Before Abraham was, I Am."—John 8:58

"Before Abraham was, I Am" is spoken by Jesus near the end of Chapter 8 in the Gospel of John. This is a Cosmic Christ moment because Jesus is rooting his life in the deep reaches of time and space, from before the time of Abraham, the founder of the Hebrew people. When does the ministry of the Christ begin?

The four Gospels in the New Testament answer this question in different ways: some with his birth and some with his baptism as an adult. But John, in the great Prologue, makes the astounding claim that this man's life and ministry was initiated from the origin of all that is. Does the meaning of this current saying, "Before Abraham was, I Am," differ from that of the Prologue?

The Prologue begins on the vast stage of the universe. By contrast, the statement "Before Abraham was, I Am" is made in the midst of a sharp back-and-forth exchange between Jesus and a group of religious leaders. Chapter 8 in John begins with the famous story of a woman who, caught in adultery, is being brought to Jesus. It is yet another attempt by his detractors to trap him—what will he say about this flagrant breach of the religious teachings? The punishment for adultery is death by stoning—will Jesus dare to let this woman off?

In addition to the dramatic unfolding story, the placement of this account is also important. The story of the woman caught in adultery was, in the early Church, a story with no fixed home. Early texts of the New Testament have it in both Luke and in John. We may think that it was a story that was inserted into a gospel narrative. Why was it placed where we find it today, at the beginning of Chapter 8 in the Gospel of John?

Looking at the chapter as a whole, introduced by this dramatic, defining story, we find that questions of identity and status are themes for the entire chapter. The assertion of the Prologue, that Christ was from the very beginning of all time and space, all things, is advanced in Chapter 8, thus helping us understand that our identity is cosmic, and not based on things like accidents of birth and personal effort.

The woman dragged before Jesus for judgment is saved by Jesus leveling the field between the woman and her accusers: "Let the one of you who is without sin cast the first stone" (John 8:7). The woman is not less, nor is she more, than the self-righteous (who may have duplicity added to their list of faults, in that it is not really interest in the woman's crime that brings them to Jesus, but an attempt to ensnare him).

By putting the Woman Caught in Adultery at the start of Chapter 8, the Gospel opens a subterranean theme that will emerge strongly as the chapter unfolds: that of Jesus' own identity. Jesus' opponents could have used any number of transgressions as a pretext for trapping him—why did they choose adultery?

These opponents knew the rumors about Jesus: that he was an illegitimate child, a bastard, conceived outside of marriage. By dragging this woman before him, Jesus' enemies hoped to rattle and destabilize him by inferring his own illegitimacy.

At one time in Jesus' life, this question would have served as a bitter reminder for him and could have shaken his confidence in his own capacity. Twentieth-century psychoanalyst Erik Erikson wrote sensitively and insightfully about what it would have been like for Jesus to grow up in a small village wherein his illegitimacy was known by all.

In Palestine at the time of Jesus, identity was closely tied to family. Think about how you would establish yourself if there were no universities or unions or business institutions to certify you and to create networks of support. Palestinian Jews relied on their family ties for their support and identity. Today we derive our identity and support more from wider societal networks than they did at that time and place. Erikson describes a very believable crisis in the life of the young Jesus, which led to a spiritual breakthrough: "My true father is God." Jesus went through an archetypal journey of transformation, going beyond the borders of the hero's quest into an essentially inner struggle that did not depend on personal strength or prowess, but on a movement of opening to a greater reality. For Jesus this greater reality was to acknowledge and align with God as with a loving father.

While Jesus made a spiritual ascent to the Divine Father, it was his Mother who helped him with his journey. This statement also surfaces the question of the guide for our journey to maturity. Beginning with Mary of Nazareth, there are women central to the story of Jesus who serve as guides. Finally, though, just as we must internalize the journey, the guide, too, must be found within.

Years later, in his manhood, Jesus finds himself in this debate about parentage that was meant to shock him. "We have Abraham as an ancestor," Jesus' enemies say. The saying, "Before Abraham was, I Am" is about our foundation in life, our "parentage." Jesus responds to his enemies by saying that the true "children of Abraham" are those who do as Abraham did, not simply blood descendants. Abraham's primary act was not an outward deed, but an act of obedience, of listening to and following the divine voice. Abraham is the paragon of those who act by faith.

We can feel in this debate that Jesus' confidence rests on an identity that came at the end of an inner quest. The New Testament often speaks of a mysterious spiritual quality called Rest. Rest is the state of being on the other side of our search for true identity.

When we stand before this statement of the Cosmic Christ, "Before Abraham was, I Am," we are given the gift of assessing where we stand. What is the basis of our identity? If all the memberships and certifications we've accumulated with such great effort were stripped away, would we have an identity? How familiar am I with the self that remains when all these common markers of identity vanish?

What is the basis of your stability? How do you identify yourself? What is your foundation for acting with confidence in the world?

This "I Am is an unsettling statement; an indication that great change is portended. The invitation is to embrace the understanding of the Cosmic Christ in "Before Abraham was, I Am"—and to become sensitive to the aspects of one's identity that are based on the call from the cosmos itself. It is an invitation to respond generously to our vocation.

2. THE EUCHARISTIC WORDS

Then he took some bread, and when he had given thanks, broke it and gave it to them, saying, "This is my body which will be given for you; do this as a memorial of me." He did the same with the cup after supper, and said, "This cup is the new covenant in my blood which will be poured out for you."

—Luke 22:19

A good argument could be made that the traditional words around the Last Supper that are employed in the Eucharistic ritual or Liturgy are "I Am" statements. In effect the words: "This is my body" said over the bread, and "This is the cup of my blood" said over the wine, are saying "I am this bread" and "I am this wine." In addition, the provocative words, "Do this in memory of me" also come very close to saying, "I am present in the memory of this sacred meal."

Memory is at the heart of Jewish liturgy, as Rabbi Heschel has written. (It is also at the heart of Sufi ritual: the word *zikr* means "to remember.") We are talking here of what British scientist Rupert Sheldrake calls "morphic resonance," which is common to all ritual and ceremony: an arousing of group memory, a bringing in of the ancestors, a calling in of the communion of saints. Vietnamese Buddhist teacher Thich Nhat Hanh understands the Eucharist in that fashion and reminds us that to invoke bread and wine in a sacramental meal of sharing is to call on the memory of the very history of the universe itself. He writes: "Not many people want to become priests in our day, but everyone is hungry. So many people are hungry for spiritual food; there are so many hungry souls." And he speaks of Jesus' words at the Last Supper reenacted in Catholic worship:

'Take, my friends, this is my flesh, this is my blood'—Can there be any more drastic language in order to wake you up? What could Jesus have said that is better than that? ... This piece of bread is the body of the whole cosmos. If Christ is the body of God, which he is, then the bread he offers is also the body of the cosmos. Look deeply and you notice the sunshine in the bread, the blue sky in the bread, the cloud and the great earth in the bread. Can you tell me what is not in a piece of bread? The whole cosmos has come together in order to bring to you this piece of bread. You eat it in such a way that you come alive, truly alive.[64]

The eating and drinking of the bread and the wine, then, is not about a cannibalistic exercise of eating the flesh of Jesus—rather, it is a Cosmic Christ experience. One is receiving fully of the sacred bread and life force of the universe itself. All is sacred, and we remember that in a group way by sharing the wine and bread as a community. What, after all, is more intimate than eating or drinking? We are eating and drinking the very sacred food and drink from the edges of the universe when we are eating and drinking this divine food.

In this context also, the sacred banquet of communion is a profound mystical experience. The late French philosopher Gaston Bachelard taught about the "Three I's"—Immensity, Intensity, and Intimacy. All mysticism and all encounters with the Cosmic Christ, it seems to me, can be understood in the context of the Three I's. There is in the Eucharist an experience of *immensity*, for one is taking in the very cosmic food that bread and wine are, as well as cosmic space and cosmic time, for it took 13.8 billion years for this bread and wine to arrive in its current form. There is also an experience of *intensity*, for one remembers such holy moments of communion—they are very difficult to forget. And one also undergoes *intimacy*, since the taking in of the Cosmic Christ in food and drink, like all eating, is an intimate experience. The food, after all, breaks up and becomes a part of us; it nourishes and supports us as we set out to become food for others. What is more intimate than food and drink becoming part of our beings, even cosmic food and cosmic drink?

This archetype hints at one of the I Am sayings discussed earlier: "I am the bread of life." It also connects to the "I Am" saying of "I am the vine," since grapes and wine come from the vine. The Christ is present not just on the vine or in the bread but in the drinking and eating of both—especially in a community context, for "where two or three are gathered in my name I am in the midst of them" (Matthew 18:20). These words, taken from the wisdom texts of the Hebrew Bible and applied in Judaism to the *shekinah* or the indwelling of God among us, remind us that community itself is a setting in which Wisdom becomes incarnate. And, we might add, edible.

THE CHRIST MANDALA

BISHOP MARC: When I walk the Stations of the Cross, I am learning what the sufferings of Christ mean, and how my own struggles are spiritually meaningful. When I walk the Stations of the Cosmic Christ, I am identifying with the cosmological powers that radiate from the living Christ. The Stations of the Cosmic Christ can also aid your spiritual life in a potent way, providing guidance and direction on your unfolding path in life, both for you as an individual and for your spiritual community. In this section we will explore how an ancient Christian practice, linked with the Cosmic Christ Stations, can support your spiritual life.

THE CHRISTIAN MANDALIC PROCESS

There are graphic representations of what I call the Mandala of Christ, or the Western Mandala. These images in mosaic, painted illuminations, and carvings use traditional symbols for each Gospel—Matthew, the

winged human; Mark, the winged lion; John, the eagle; and Luke, the winged bull—in what I call the Western mandalic order (Matthew, Mark, John, Luke), and they surround an image of Christ. Here is a ninth-century Western mandala from an illuminated Bible.

Working independently, Dr. Alexander Shaia and Father Bruno Barnhart have uncovered Christian spiritual practices that shaped individual and community lives for most of the first millennium of Christianity. Dr. Shaia believes that Christian Baptism involved a four-part path of personal and communal transformation, each part associated with one of the Gospels in the New Testament: Matthew, Mark, Luke, and John. In the season of Baptism (before and after Easter), the Gospels were used in a different order than at other times: Matthew, Mark, John, and Luke.

- The Gospel of Matthew was associated with the question, "How do I accept change?"
- The Gospel of Mark was associated with the question, "How do I cope with suffering?"
- The Gospel of John was associated with the question, "How do I receive blessing?"
- The Gospel of Luke was associated with the question, "How do I serve the world?"

Barnhart, in his wise book on the Gospel of John, *The Good Wine: Reading John From the Center*, argues that this Gospel has a narrative shape like a mandala: that it has a center from which the story radiates out in the four directions.

Together Shaia and Bruno have described what I call a mandalic process, a spiritual path that spirals toward the center—or Christ—with Matthew and Mark and John; and with Luke it spirals outwards toward the surrounding world. A word needs to be said about John. The symbol of the Gospel of John is the eagle; the only one of the four symbolic creatures who is naturally winged. Spiritually speaking, the experience of entering the world of the Gospel of John is one of expansiveness. Of the four stopping places along the spiral, John is the closest to the Christ center. The "I Am" statements unique to John serve as bridges from change and suffering into blessedness and the experience of the resurrected Christ in the center.

The Mandala in Hinduism and Buddhism

How is the mandala we call the Mandala of Christ or the Western Mandala like the much better-known mandalas of Hinduism and Buddhism? The mandala in Hinduism and Buddhism is a basic geometric figure of a circle containing a square, with a strong center usually occupied by a god or goddess.

Various spiritual practices evolved around mandalas in Hinduism and Buddhism. A widely understood practice is to meditate on the mandala, taking a spiral journey through the field around the center, meeting the various subsidiary beings on the way; at the center, one receives the qualities of the central divinity. The spiral journey to the center of the mandala in Buddhism and Hinduism parallels the personal and communal transformation process in early Christianity described by Shaia and Bruno.

Psychoanalysis and the Mandala

The great 20th-century psychoanalyst C.G. Jung recognized that mandalas were sometimes generated—in dreams or in artwork while working with therapists—by patients who had shattering experiences, people who needed to find a center. These mandalas were graphically like those formally produced within religious contexts. They had the dynamic of the mandalic process, of moving through suffering toward healing and the eventual restoration of a life in the world. Dr. Jung beautifully described this process of the wounded psyche as "Nature seeking to heal itself" by providing a center for a scattered, traumatized life.

As a rule, a mandala occurs in conditions of psychic dissociation or disorientation. For instance, in the case of children between the ages of eight and eleven whose parents are about to be divorced; or in adults who, as the result of a neurosis and its treatment, are confronted with the problem of opposites in human nature and are consequently disoriented; or again in schizophrenics whose view of the world has become confused, owing to the invasion of incomprehensible contents from the unconscious. In such cases it is easy to see how the severe pattern imposed by a circular image of this kind compensates the disorder and confusion of the psychic state—namely, through the construction of a central point to which everything is related, or by a concentric arrangement of the disordered multiplicity and of contradictory and irreconcilable elements. This is evidently an attempt at self-healing on the part of nature, which does not spring from conscious reflection but from an instinctive impulse.

There are many forces that tear apart and break the integrity of the whole. Dr. Jung suggests that the mandala is a tool of Nature—and I would say of God—to heal that which is broken. The spontaneous appearance of mandalas is a manifestation of grace in our lives. It is important to remember that making mandalas in a conscious way, within a religious tradition, is not less graceful than those spontaneously produced, but rather is an example of the human will working in harmony with the grace of God.

Here is another Western mandala, from a Spanish Bible, with figures in the circular field surrounding the Lamb of God, a symbol of Christ.

Beatus of Llébana is offering a commentary on the Apocalypse (left), Spanish, 10th century

Dr. Shaia believes that what I call the mandalic process in Christianity was lost by the eighth century. The graphic examples I have found, like the previous two above, suggest that the process was remembered in some places for several hundred years more. But nevertheless, by our own time the process had been forgotten. As with the mandala in Hinduism and Buddhism, the spiritual practices around the Western mandala probably varied from place to place as well as over time. In addition, the details of how the processes worked have been lost.

Matthew Fox and Bishop Marc Andrus

The needs the Western mandala addressed—personal and communal healing, transformation, and guidance in the spiritual journey—have not vanished. The Western mandala has reemerged at the time it is most needed, when we are facing planetary crisis, when so many on the globe are living in extreme poverty, and when the soul of the West has been brutalized by materialism and objectification.

Stations of the Cosmic Christ can be used with the Western mandala to provide fresh spiritual practice that serves individual and community needs for healing and for guidance. The images can be placed in the framework of the Western mandala and be read as a momentary expression of the spiritual position of the person or community.

THE CONTEMPORARY PRACTICE OF THE MANDALA OF CHRIST

A key piece to using the Cosmic Christ Stations in the Mandala of Christ framework is the idea of synchronicity. The idea of synchronicity differs from the idea of causality. In the contemporary world we look for causes and effects, but wisdom practices of both East and West have depended on ideas of synchronicity and interconnectedness. Carl Jung, in his introduction to Richard Wilhelm's translation of the *I Ching*, wrote this about synchronicity:

> Whoever invented the I Ching was convinced that the hexagram worked out in a certain moment coincided with the latter in quality no less than in time. To him the hexagram was the exponent of the moment in which it was cast—even moreso than the hours of the clock or the divisions of the calendar could be—inasmuch as the hexagram was understood to be an indicator of the essential situation prevailing in the moment of its origin.

This assumption involves a certain curious principle: synchronicity, a concept that formulates a point of view diametrically opposed to that of causality. Since causality is a merely statistical truth and not absolute, it is a sort of working hypothesis of how events evolve one out of another. Synchronicity, however, takes the coincidence of events in space and time as meaning something more than mere chance. It indicates a peculiar interdependence of objective events among themselves, as well as with the subjective (psychic) states of the observer or observers.

The first step in the spiritual practice of the Mandala of Christ is to create hand-size images of the 16 Stations of the Cosmic Christ. You could purchase the accompanying prayer cards for this book, you could make your own images, or you could search for representations in art. Here is one that I use to represent "I Am he, Jesus of Nazareth":

With a prayerful intention you would select one of the 16 Cosmic Christ Stations to occupy the center of the mandala you are creating. You are selecting a central image, the equivalent to the Christ in Glory at the center of what I have called the Western mandala (Christ surrounded by the symbols of the four Gospels). This selection for the center of the mandala is your intellectual/emotional/spiritual contribution to the synchronous moment that is represented by the final mandala; the other four cards will be drawn at random from the full deck of prayer cards, trusting the unfolding of a meaningful pattern, responding to your prayerful intent.

Draw four cards—one at a time—that bear the images of other Stations, and array them around the central figure, moving clockwise. The result will be the Mandala of the Stations of Christ. Simply gaze at this mandala, and hold the following life questions of the mandalic process in your heart:

Place the first card above the central figure (in the position of the north). The associated question is, "How do I respond to change?" the question associated with the first Gospel, the Gospel of Matthew. Sit with this question and the image that you have drawn. What comes to mind as you think about change in your life, and the symbolic meanings of the selected image? After quietly reflecting on the question of change and the image the moment has given you, look at that central image (which you chose) paired with the image you have drawn from the deck. How does the association of these two images enrich your meditation?

Next draw a second card by random selection and place it to the right of the central image (in the position of the east). This image corresponds to the life question, "How do I deal with suffering?" and the second Gospel, the Gospel of Mark. The question of suffering is a difficult one to sit with quietly, to keep our minds patiently focused on the question of suffering—here more than anywhere we find our minds moving to other topics. Gently return, perhaps using your breath paired with the question, "How do I deal with suffering?" to return to this topic.

After you have sat with the question of suffering for a while, link this question to the first one, "How do I deal with change?" and then with the central image.

After you have meditated on the central image, on change, and on suffering, draw another card from the face-down prayer deck. This card, carrying the life question, "How do I receive blessing?" (the central question of the Gospel of John), is placed below the central figure, in the place of south. You may find that there is an inner resistance to staying with the question of blessing, perhaps even as much as with the question of suffering. Sometimes we don't feel worthy to receive blessing. It is worth going deeper when we encounter a resistance to acknowledging blessing in our lives. What is the source of this resistance?

After meditating on blessing, go back, stepwise, through suffering, change, and the central image, holding the whole emerging pattern before you, and asking what greater light of understanding is dawning.

Finally, draw one more card from the down-turned deck, the card associated with the question, "How do I serve?" (the life question of the Gospel of Luke). Place this last card to the left of the central image in the place of west. The question of service is an exciting one. Service represents purpose and meaning for many people. Even contemplatives, people who devote their lives to quiet prayer, often in seclusion, characterize this sequestered life as a life of service. The famous Zen painting series, the *Oxherding Series*, ends with a painting of the Zen practitioner as an ox laboring in the world, serving humanity and the world. How are you being called to serve? What service draws on your particular skills, interests, and abilities? How are you being called to serve *in this moment*?

After reflecting on the question of service, the opportunity is open to contemplate the whole, completed mandala, the central image you chose, surrounded by the four prayer cards you drew trusting in the moment. You may wish to repeat the pattern of mentally building the mandala in a stepwise fashion that was used with the previous prayer cards: begin with the last card you drew (the one in the west, "How do I serve?") and going backwards through "How do I receive blessing?" to "How do I deal with suffering?" to "How do I deal with change?" and at last to the central image. After working your way backwards from the image associated with "How do I serve?" to the central image, you will have mentally built the whole Mandala of Christ. What is the message that comes to you through the completed mandala?

What follows is an example of the Mandala of the Stations of the Christ practice. In this example, based on a prayerful openness to God's direction, a decision was made to choose "I Am He, the One You are Seeking" as the central image.

The four Stations that emerged in the moment of prayer were as follows: Resurrection (Change); I Am the Light (Suffering); I Am the Way, the Truth and the Life (Blessing); and Pentecost (Service). Rather than using the images we have provided in this book as exemplars or prototypes of the Cosmic Christ Stations, I searched for images that came from the art of early Christianity, bearing in mind that for much of the first 1,000 years of Christianity, the mandalic process was in use in some areas of the Middle East and Northern Africa, as well as in Ireland, France, and Germany. The images I found follow, in their mandalic order.

RESURRECTION

Resurrection, Rabbula Gospels Book, Syria, Sixth Century

The first image, Resurrection (Change) comes from a remarkable and early book of Gospels, the Rabbula Gospels, created in Syria in the sixth century. Pairing the idea of accepting change (Matthew's question) with the image of Resurrection was fruitful. Christians understand resurrection to be distinct from resuscitation.

Resuscitation is the resumption of an interrupted life (someone brought back from near-drowning, for instance, who goes back to her job and her family, shaken but able to resume the threads of her life). Resurrection, however, is a qualitative change of being, a translation to another plane of existence. Where is resurrection showing up in my life now? Am I holding myself back from profound change? If so, why?

The Rabbula Gospels' depiction of the Resurrection includes several scenes from the New Testament related to the raising of Jesus from the dead. The scenes are organized differently than Western graphic narration, in that the story is read from the middle of the picture, rather than from left to right. Thus, we see the guards of the tomb struck down by amazement in the center, in front of the tomb—the door of which stands open. To the left are the women who come to mourn Jesus and anoint his body. An angel tells them that Jesus is not here but has risen. To the right of the picture, we see Jesus himself speaking with the worshipful women. The details of this painting identify the New Testament source as being the Gospel of Matthew, the gospel associated with the question of change.

"I Am the Light" (Suffering)

The association of light with suffering is jarring and discordant at first. Light is associated with benediction, new beginnings, and understanding. Suffering obscures and distorts our lives, or so we think at first. But

suffering is a kind of light, or it can bring light. Many people have found that in retrospect they learned more through periods of opposition, suffering, and pain than in times of prosperity and normalcy. We often discover inner resources that we did not know were there. Communities come to our aid; friends show up. All of this may be called a kind of light. The image I chose here for the Station of "I Am the Light of the World" is an ancient mosaic from the cathedral in Monreale, Sicily, dating from the late 12th century.

Christ is seen against a shining golden background, which represents eternity. His right hand is held up in blessing, and in his left hand is a Bible, open to the verse of the Gospel of John that says, "I Am the Light of the World."

"I Am the Way, the Truth, and the Life (Blessing)"

The Greek word for truth conveys that it is not a substance ("I have the truth;" "These people don't know the truth"), but is a gateway to that which is real. Truth understood as opening is contrasted with blockages in our thinking, places of being stuck. A reality so different from the one in which we are suffering through wrong perceptions is available across the most gossamer of veils, but it might as well be through a solid mountain as long as we accept the barrier as real and the suffering on this side of the barrier as ultimate. With truth being an opening, we understand that this Station describes the spiritual path. Like others among the Stations, it says that Christ is a being who contains a comprehensive, complex reality: not just the path, but the gateway to blessedness, and the state of blessedness itself. This Station, associated with blessing, asks me to see where blessing is close by, but perhaps not appreciated or apprehended.

The image here for "I Am the Way, the Truth, and the Life" is another mosaic, this one from a church of late antiquity in Ravenna, about 600 years older than the Monreale mosaic.

Christ in this mosaic is dressed like a Byzantine emperor. Instead of a crown, however, a halo surrounds Christ's head, and he holds neither spear nor scepter, but a cross in his right hand. In his left is not a shield, but the Gospel of John's verse, "I Am the Way, the Truth, and the Life," in Latin. Christ's face has a calm about it, and he holds us with a steady, kindly gaze.

PENTECOST (SERVICE)

The Feast of Pentecost is the Christian observance of a story in the Acts of the Apostles. The Spirit of God, no longer resting on a single human being, spread among the early believers in what then was called the Way. It is striking that the Book of the Acts of the Apostles describes these early Christians as caring for the poor and sick. The gift of the Spirit at Pentecost enabled the Christians to be courageous and compassionate. Pentecost and service are closely associated. The conjunction of this station with the question, "How do I serve?" helps me look at opportunities to serve in collaboration, as part of a body, rather than making only an individual effort.

We return to the Rabbula Gospels for the image for this Station of the Cosmic Christ. What I love about this miniature of the Pentecost is that Mary, the mother of Jesus, has been placed at the center of the community of the believers (who are all men). The Rabbula Gospels are not singular in depicting Pentecost with Mary at the center; however, her presence is not mentioned in the canonical New Testament Gospels. This image adds to our understanding of the event by making the idea of the Body of Christ, the community of the believers, one that includes both women and men.

CONCLUSION TO THE MANDALA OF CHRIST PRACTICE

The highest order of meditation is to look at the mandala as a whole and seek to see how it speaks to the moment in which you and your community find yourselves, with the past and future bound up in the present moment too.

Viewing the whole Mandala of Christ that you have created by the combination of a conscious choice (the selection of the central image) and by trust in the providence of a living universe (the drawing of four cards from the face-down deck of prayer cards) is a symbolic vision of your whole self. When we are in the middle of an intense experience that is dominated by one of the four life questions (change, suffering, blessing, service) it may be very challenging to see that the substance of the other questions has not vanished--they are still with us, still part of us. Meditation on the Mandala of Christ may reveal to us more of our complete self, a self that the dominant life question at the time may obscure.

The central figure, the one you chose at the beginning of making a new Mandala of Christ, also bears a spiritual possibility for you, a rare opportunity to glimpse the deeper aspects of your inner life. In your heart, at the core of your being, the Cosmic Christ shines. The selection you made of the central image was conditioned by the deepest wells of your life, the light shining in the darkness. The prayerful selection of this image is a grace-filled moment, a gift from the Cosmic Christ who is within you, showing you this luminous aspect of yourself.

The practice of creating a Mandala of Christ using these prayer cards is one that can be repeated at points in your life when you are seeking guidance. The Mandala of Christ is also a spiritual practice that can be used by a community, the same life questions being applied to the life of the community rather than the life of an individual person.

The selection of these images themselves is a spiritual practice. The images that inspired our book, *The Stations of the Cosmic Christ*, were the original work of two artists, M.C. Richards and Ullrrich Javier Lemus. Since Matthew and I led the first workshop on the Stations of the Cosmic Christ in 2013, several people around the world have been inspired to create their own images for the Stations. You should feel encouraged to make your own prayer cards of the Stations of the Cosmic Christ as a further means of using the Stations as spiritual practice.

3. CHANTING CHRISTIAN MANTRAS

FOX: For several years now I have been creating mantras from the Christian tradition and inviting people to chant them with me. The effects have often been profound. One group of Protestant clergy said that the experience kept them up all night afterwards! It is one thing to study the Scriptures and think and meditate and preach about them—and it is a totally other thing to chant them as mantras. A mantra is a device that is repeated over and over again. Think bumper sticker: Short, pithy sayings from Jesus or the Christ or the mystics. In this sense a rosary is a mantra, and a litany is one also, for repetition is at their core. It is time to take meaningful sayings from the sources of our Western heritage and chant them—not think about them or debate them or even study them, though that has its place—but to chant them over and over. This practice is a powerful exercise for the right brain, which learns more from chanting and the rhythm it creates than from thinking about things.

The following are examples of mantras that can be employed, although I encourage people to create their own as well. Mantras are very portable, very accessible, very approachable. They are a fitting way to exercise our mystical awareness, especially in this time when people are very busy and need practices that are readily available.

- The "I Am" sayings found in this book. For example, "I Am the Vine," "I Am the Door," "I Am the Living Light," and so on. Simply chant them over and over alone or with others and see what happens.
- Words from Jesus' mouth, such as, "The Kingdom of God is within you," and "The Queendom of God is among you," both of which are accurate translations. Or: "Do it to the least and you do it to me." Or "Love your enemy." "Take and eat, this is my body." There is no shortage of possibilities for those who derive great benefit from the Scriptures.
- Short phrases from the mystics can be very powerful. For example, one might chant one of the following phrases from Meister Eckhart:

"Is-ness is God."

"Compassion is where peace and justice kiss."

"God finds joy and rapture in us."

From Julian of Norwich, one might chant:

"Goodness is God."

"All will be well."

"Jesus says: 'I am what you love.'"

"Jesus says: 'I am what you serve.'"

From Hildegard of Bingen, one might chant:

"Limitless love, from the depths to the stars: flooding all, loving all."

"Become a flowering orchard."

"Mary, ground of all being."

"Love was the first. She made everything."

From Mechtild of Magdeburg, one might chant:

"Kneel at the feet of all creatures."

"You, God, are the sun: I am your reflection."

"I was created in love."

4. CHANTING THE "AH" SOUND AMONG DIVINE NAMES

A practice in interfaith or Deep Ecumenism

Sit in a chair with feet on the floor so breath can move easily. Chant the sound "Ah" for several minutes. Then chant the following mantras, repeating each one several times, and emphasize the "Ah" sound in each:

Aum
Buddha
Brahmin
Krishna
Tara
Gaia
Shiva
Shakti
Kali
Yahweh
Adonai
Sophia
Hochmah
Allah
Tagashala
Wakan Tanka
Abba

The "Ah" sound is common to so many divine names around the world. To speak or chant it is to open the fourth and fifth chakras. Thus this is a practice in Deep Ecumenism. "Abba" was Jesus' favorite name for the Divine; it means "Father" or "Papa."

5. THE 16 STATIONS DEPICTED BY ARTISTS FROM ITALY AND POLAND

BY MACIEJ BIELAWSKI

The Baptism

The Living Bread

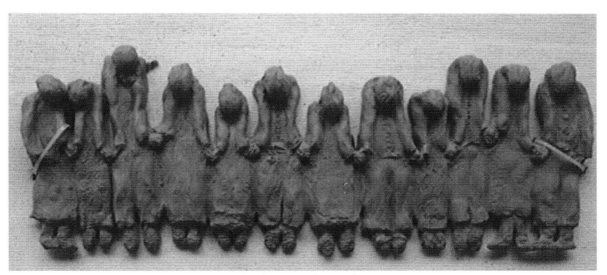

Do it to the least and you do it to me.

I Am the Door.

COSMIC CHRIST TOTEM

The Cosmic Christ

2001 John Tracy, carver

MATTHEW FOX AND BISHOP MARC ANDRUS

To me, the Cosmic Christ is a reflection and model of the interconnection of individual and collective uniqueness as a creative process. The Christ is individual (male and female), collective, center, into, and from which flow the water and bread of life through the invisible channels, which link us all.

This totem is carved according to spiritual totem tradition from around the globe. Most spiritual totems are a personification of the interconnection of all aspects of spirit as seen in a given culture. Each culture, tribe, family, and individual tend to use specific symbols (usually animal, bird, or flower) to represent these spiritual centers and powers.

Starting from the bottom, key features of the totem include the Star of David in which the totem sits, eternal symbols of God found in most indigenous cultures, the primordial waters from which the four elements arise (fire, earth, air, and water are depicted on each side of the lower section), the four directions represented by each side of the totem, the tree of life, and the river of life (blue beads just under the turtle). The turtle represents Mother Earth and the root chakra …

The next major level is the human manifest consciousness as represented in the head of Jesus. Here we have also the third eye, the crown chakra, which is linked to the higher consciousness of Christ, represented in the figurine emerging from and into the entire creation. This figurine is not a cross. It is the blessing Christ, the risen Christ, the Holy Spirit, and the invisible channels which link the consciousness of all life with each other and with the mind of God.

The Totem was blessed in a sacred ceremony with sacred water, sacred sounds, the blood of the carver (while carving), and prayer. I pray that whoever looks upon or touches the Cosmic Christ in faith shall also be blessed and healed of their wounds of estrangement, disease, and fears.

The figurine of the Blessing Christ came from a dream in which I was walking and speaking with Jesus in a small mountain village plaza. At a rock garden at the edge of the village, Jesus reached into one of his many coats, took out the figurine, placed it on a rock, and said, "Pray with me."

—John Tracy

SACRED SCRIPTURE PASSAGES BEHIND THE STATIONS OF THE COSMIC CHRIST

• Station One: "In the beginning was the ... Word ... Fireball ... Flaring Forth ... Big Bang ... Void ..." See Genesis 1:1; John 1:1.

• Station Two: "I Am the Light of the World." See John 1:4-14; 7:12; 9:1-39; 12:35-36, 40; Matthew 5:14-16; Genesis 1:3-4.

• Station Three: Nativity. See Matthew 1:1-17; Luke 2:1-20.

• Station Four: "I Am the Living Bread." See John 6:1; Isaiah 25:6; Matthew 26:26-29; Luke 22:19f; Mark 14:22-24; 1 Corinthians 11:23-32.

• Station Five: The Baptism: See Mark 1:9-13; Matthew 3:13-11; Acts 10:38; Isaiah 64:1.

• Station Six: The Transfiguration: See Matthew 17:1-8; Mark 9:2-9; Luke 9:28-36; 2 Peter 1:16-18; Exodus 19:3-25; 33:18-21.

• Station Seven: "I Am the Vine." See John 15:1-17; Matthew 20:1-8; 21:28-41; Isaiah 5:1-10; Jerimiah 2:21,12:10; Ezekial 19:10.
• Station Eight: "Do it to the least and you do it to me." See Matthew 25:31-46.

• Station Nine: "I Am the good shepherd." See John 10:1-18.

• Station 10: "I Am the door (the gate, the way)." See John 10:9-10; Matthew 7:13-14.

• Station 11: "I Am the Way, the Truth, and the Life." See John 14:5-21.

• Station 12: The Crucifixion. See Mark 15:33-39; Matthew 27:45-54; Luke 23:44-48.

- Station 13: The Resurrection. See Matthew 28:1-20; Mark 16:1-20; Luke 24:1-49; John 20:1-18.

- Station 14: "I Am the Resurrection and the Life." See John 11:1-44.

- Station 15: Ascension. See Luke 24:50-53; Mark 16:19-20; Acts 1:2-14; Ephesians 4:3-16.

- Station 16: Pentecost. See Acts. 2:1-47; John 20:19-29.

ENDNOTES

1. Rollo May, *The Cry for Myth* (New York: Delta, 1991), 29
2. Burton L. Mack, *The Lost Gospel: The Book of Q & Christian Origins* (San Francisco: HarperSanFrancisco, 1994), 125
3. William Hermanns, *Einstein and the Poet: In Search of the Cosmic Man* (Brookline Village, MA: Branden Press, Inc., 1983), 68-69
4. Teilhard de Chardin, *Writings in Time of War* (New York: Harper &Row, 1968), 262
5. Pierre Teilhard de Chardin, *Human Energy* (New York: A Harvest/HBJ Book, 1969), 23, 130
6. D. E. Nineham, *Saint Mark* (London: Penguin, 1979), 235
7. Matthew Fox, *The Coming of the Cosmic Christ* (San Francisco: HarperSanFrancisco, 1988), 107
8. I am indebted to the late French philosopher Gaston Bachelard for the naming of what I call the "three i's." See Gaston Bachelard, *The Poetics of Space: The Classic Look at How We Experience Intimate Places* (Boston: Beacon Press, 1994)
9. Matthew Fox, *Passion for Creation: The Earth-Honoring Spirituality of Meister Eckhart* (Rochester, Vermont, Inner Traditions, 1991), 429, 435f
10. M.C. Richards, *Opening Our Moral Eye: Essays, Talks, & Poems Embracing Creativity & Community* (Hudson, New York: Lindisfarne Press, 1996), 44f
11. Ibid., 48
12. S. Staubach, "Imagine Inventing Yellow, The Life and Works of M.C. Richards, Exhibition Catalog," (Worcester, Massachusetts: Worcester Center for Crafts, 1999), 20f
13. Richards, *Opening Our Moral Eye*, 120f
14. Ibid., 121
15. M.C. Richards, *Centering in Pottery, Poetry, and the Person* (Middletown, Ct: Wesleyan University Press, 1964), 60. xvi Ibid., 107
16. Ibid., 107
17. Howard Thurman, *The Search for Common Ground* (Richmond, Indiana: Friends United Press, 1986), 8
18. Ibid, 107
19. Brendan Doyle, *Meditations with Julian of Norwich* (Santa Fe, NM: Bear & Co., 1983), 69, 74
20. Sue Woodruff, *Meditations with Mechtild of Magdeburg*, (Santa Fe, NM: Bear & Co., 1982), 71
21. Fox, *Passion for Creation* (Rochester, Vermont: Inner Traditions, 1991), 111-113
22. Ibid., 217
23. Cited in Matthew Fox, *Hildegard of Bingen's Book of Divine Works with Letters and Songs* (Santa Fe: Bear & Co., 1987), 308-310
24. M.C. Richards, *Imagine Inventing Yellow: New and Selected Poems* (Barrytown, NY: Station Hill, 1991), 30
25. Richards, *Centering in Pottery, Poetry, and the Person*, 139
26. Ibid., 147
27. See Matthew Fox, *One River, Many Wells: Wisdom Springing from Global Faiths* (New York: Jeremy P. Tarcher/Putnam, 2000), 50-79
28. Matthew Fox, *Sins of the Spirit, Blessings of the Flesh: Transforming Evil in Soul and Society* (Berkeley, CA: North

Atlantic Press, 2016), 50-57

29. John O'Donohue, *Anam Cara: A Book of Celtic Wisdom* (New York: HarperCollins, 1997), 4f

30. Gabriele Uhlein, *Meditations with Hildegard of Bingen* (Santa Fe: Bear & Co., 1982), 70

31. Fox, *Passion for Creation*, 289

32. Thich Naht Hanh, *Living Buddha, Living Christ* (New York: Riverhead, 1995), 145

33. Daniel Ladinsky, trans., *The Gift: Poems by Hafiz, the Great Sufi Master* (New York: Arkana, 1999), 159

34. See Fox, *Passion for Creation*, 335-337

35. See Erich Jantsch, *The Self-Organizing Universe* (New York: Pergamon Press, 1980), 308 where Jantsch calls God "the mind of the universe."

36. Richards, *Imagine Inventing Yellow*, 4

37. Neil Douglas Klotz, *Prayers of the Cosmos: Meditations on the Aramaic Words of Jesus* (San Francisco: Harper & Row Publishers, 1990), 26

38. The Didache, Part 9 of the Eucharist, instituteofcatholicculture.org/wp-content/uploads/2012/06/The_Didache_Handout.pdf

39. Leonard Doohan, *Mark: Visionary of Early Christianity* (Santa Fe, NM: Bear & Co., 1986), 90

40. Richards, *Opening Our Moral Eye*, 45

41. Ibid

42. Paul Lukacs, *Inventing Wine: A New History on One of the World's Most Ancient Pleasures* (New York: W. W. Norton & Co, 2012), 25f

43. Ibid., 27

44. Ibid

45. Doyle, *Meditations with Julian of Norwich*, 84

46. Martin Luther King, Jr., "Out of the Long Night," in *The Gospel Messenger*, Feb 8, 1958 (Elgin, Illinois, Official Organ of the Church of the Brethren), 14

47. Fox, *Passion for Creation*, 523

48. Richards, *Opening Our Moral Eye*, 134

49. Ibid., 45 and Staubach, *Imagine Inventing Yellow Exhibition Catalog*, 21

50. Richards, *Opening Our Moral Eye*, 129

51. Bachelard, *The Poetics of Space*, 212

52. Ibid., 3

53. Richards, *Opening Our Moral Eye*, 45

54. Doyle, *Meditations with Julian of Norwich*, 44

55. See Alan Light, *The Holy or the Broken: Leonard Cohen, Jeff Buckley & the Unlikely Ascent of "HALLELUJAH"* (New York: Atria Books, 2012)

56. Edward Schillebeeckx, *Christ: The Experience of Jesus as Lord* (New York: Seabury Press, 1980), 200

57. See Matthew Fox, *Sheer Joy: Conversations with Thomas Aquinas on Creation Spirituality* (New York: Jeremy P. Tarcher, 2003), 360-364

58. Julia Connor, ed., *Backpacking in the Hereafter: Poems by M.C. Richards* (Asheville, North Carolina: Black Mountain College Museum & Arts Center, 2014), 31f

59. John Shelby Spong, *The Fourth Gospel: Tales of a Jewish Mystic* (New York: HarperOne, 2013), 295

60. Thomas Berry and Brian Swimme, *The Universe Story: From the Primordial Flaring Forth to the Ecozoic Age* (San Francisco: HarperOne, 1992), 8

61. John has preserved clear evidence that Jesus saw himself as a high priest in the tradition of the temple mystics. See Margaret Barker, *Temple Mysticism : An Introduction* (London: SPCK, 2011), 350-351. Thus Jesus prayed: "Keep them in thy Name, which thou hast given me, that they may be one, even as we are one." (John 17.11). Through his disciples, Jesus would extend this unity. See ibid., 364-365.

62. The story of the anointing of David to replace King Saul is a richly meaningful story found in the Old Testament—I Samuel 16. In it the editorial note, "People judge by outward appearances, but God sees the human heart," is made, an early religious statement about the reality and great value of the inner life.

63. Luke 2:19. The verb I have translated here as *clashed* is usually translated as *pondered*, which does not get at the sense of the strong, somewhat violent verb.

64. Thich Naht Hanh, *Going Home: Jesus and Buddha as Brothers* (New York: Riverhead Books, 1999), 107

ABOUT THE AUTHORS AND ARTISTS

BISHOP MARC ANDRUS

Marc Andrus is the Eighth Bishop of the Episcopal Diocese of California. Marc is married to science manager and public health administrator, Dr. Sheila Andrus. Marc and Sheila have two daughters, Pilar and Chloé.

Marc is a leading voice in the religious world in areas of justice, particularly eco-justice, immigration, peace, LGBTQ rights, racial reconciliation, and gender equality.

While serving as Bishop of California, Marc is pursuing a doctorate in philosophy, cosmology, and consciousness at the California Institute of Integral Studies to deepen his ability to engage the planetary challenge of human-induced climate change.

MATTHEW FOX

Matthew Fox, who holds a doctorate in the history and theology of spiritualities from the Institut Catholique de Paris, is author of 35 books on spirituality and culture that have been translated into 69 languages and received many awards. A partial list of these books is offered at the front of this book. Since learning of the Creation Spirituality tradition from his mentor in Paris, French historian Pere M.D. Chenu, Fox has dedicated his life to recovering that lineage and bringing it alive. Accordingly he founded graduate programs in Culture and Creation Spirituality at colleges in Chicago and then Oakland and developed a cutting edge educational pedagogy that includes artists, scientists, mystics of all traditions, and activists to teach spirituality that includes intellect and intuition, body, heart, and mind.

Since Creation Spirituality is both a mystical and a prophetic tradition, Fox's support of women and gay rights, of the environment and social, racial, and gender justice, and of liberation theology disturbed naysayers in the Vatican, which silenced him for a year and then pressured the Dominican Order, to which he was a member for 34 years, to dismiss him.

Subsequently, he founded the University of Creation Spirualty (UCS) in Oakland, California, and became an episcopal priest to work with young people to create a postmodern worship form called *the Cosmic Mass,* which incorporates dance, dj, vj, rap and other postmodern art forms. Most recently he has co-founded an *Order of the Sacred Earth,* which is a spiritual (not religious) order open to people of all traditions and none, who feel called to focus their commitment to save the earth with a common vow to be "the best lover and the best defender of earth that I can be." A new school called the Fox Institute for Creation Spirituality has recently been launched in Boulder, Colorado, by some of the graduates of UCS.

Fox is a visiting scholar with the Academy of the Love of Learning in Santa Fe, New Mexico, founded by Leonard Bernstein and Aaron Stern. He lives in the Bay Area in Northern California. Among the awards granted him have been the Gandhi-King-Ikeda Peace Award from Morehouse College, the Humanities Award of the Sufi International Association of Sufism, the Tikkun Ethics Award, and the Courage of Conscience Award from the Peace Abbey of Sherborn, Massachusetts. Other recipients of this award include the Dalai Lama, Mother Teresa, Rosa Parks, Ernesto Cardinale, and Maya Angelou (see *matthewfox.org*).

M.C. RICHARDS (1916-1999)

M.C. Richards was a renowned potter, a beloved teacher, a challenging essayist, and an accomplished poet. Among her books are the classic *Centering in Pottery, Poetry, and the Person*; *The Crossing Point: Selected Talks and Writings*; *Toward Wholeness: Rudolf Steiner Education in America*; *Imagine Inventing Yellow: New and Selected Poems*; and *Opening Our Moral Eye*. Her seven "I Am" clay tablets were on exhibit in Carmel, California, when they caught Matthew Fox's eye at the time he was contemplating his book, *The Coming of the Cosmic Christ*. He credits her tablets with inspiring that book.

M.C. held a doctorate in English literature from the University of California at Berkeley, but she chose to abandon a prestigious position at the University of Chicago after just one year because she felt the soul was left out of mainstream academia. Instead of renewing her contract, she fled to teach at the experimental Black Mountain College in North Carolina alongside such people as Buckminster Fuller, John Cage, and Merce Cunningham, all of whom remained lifetime friends. She was a tireless advocate for education by way of art and creativity, and found an educational home as part of Matthew Fox's creation spirituality faculty at Holy Names College in Oakland, and then with the University of Creation Spirituality for many years. She lived the last 14 years of her life (when she was not on the road teaching) at Camphill Village in Kimberton Hills, Pennsylvania, an agriculture-based community for persons with developmental disabilities that was inspired by the teachings of Rudolf Steiner.

ULLRRICH JAVIER GARCIA LEMUS

Ullrrich Javier Garcia Lemus was born in El Salvador and came of age during the Contra Wars and the murder of Archbishop Romero. As a young man he received a bachelor's from the Universidad Technological de El Salvador, San Salvador, El Salvador, and worked for three years on sculpture restoration with the renowned Santiago Avila. For two years he underwent a painting tutorial with Sarakai and in 1987 he received the prestigious award for Best Sculptor and Painter at the Universidad Technologica de El Salvador.

He moved to San Francisco in 1989 and has been living there ever since, committed to his painting—which is often described as surrealistic—and his sculpting. In 2006 he was the subject of an award-winning film for the San Francisco Latino Film Festival called "Layers of Javier," which included a commentary by Dr. Matthew Fox. For a number of years he was Artist in Residence with Friends of Creation Spirituality. Included among his exhibits are the National Theater in El Salvador in 1987, La Raza gallery in San Francisco in 1994, and the Historic Sweets Ballroom, Oakland, from 1997–2006. His web page is *ullrrich.com*.

ACKNOWLEDGEMENTS

We wish to acknowledge our debt to Unity Books and Jill Angelo in particular for preparing this book for a paperback edition. Jill's support and encouragement have been especially valuable. To Ellen Debenport of Unity World Headquarters for her careful editing of this new edition, we express our gratitude. We are hopeful that the Stations of the Cosmic Christ can now reach a broad and eager audience who understands the need to move from an anthropocentric focus in religion to a more cosmic one.

At the same time we want to thank Kermit Heartsong of Tayen Lane Publishing, who produced the original handsome hardback edition and who chose Mark Serr to photograph so wonderfully the marvelous tablets that are presented in these pages. A special thanks to M.C. Richards and Ullrrich Javier Lemus for their powerful renderings of ancient archetypes and storied events into the clay icons pictured here. And to Maciej Bielawski for his painting icon and to Paola Paulini, both of Verona, Italy, for her clay tablets reproduced near the end of the book. Also to John Tracy for his gift to us all of the Totem of the Cosmic Christ.

Thanks also to Dean Malcolm Young of Grace Cathedral for his hospitality and Ray Bussolari for creating the vitrines for these icons that were installed at the Cathedral and now many other venues. A special shout-out to Dennis Edwards and John Poe for transporting, storing, setting up, and taking down these vitrines in many locations.

CARDS FOR MEDITATION

We are pleased to announce that cards for praying the Stations of the Cosmic Christ are available as well. The set of 16 cards matches the 16 icons in this book, each with an accompanying prayer and questions for reflection. These cards will make this new but ancient practice of walking the cosmic stations ever more practical and portable—use them while on the road, at home, on a plane, train, or subway. Find the cards at *shopunity.org* or call 816-251-3561. They are also available on Amazon, and retailers may order through distributors New Leaf, Ingram, and Devorss.

YOUR CHURCH, RETREAT CENTER, OR CHAPEL CAN NOW POST YOUR OWN 16 STATIONS OF THE COSMIC CHRIST

The 16 Stations in this book, created by artists M.C. Richards and Ullrrich Javier Lemus, have been displayed at Grace Cathedral in San Francisco, Trinity Church in Santa Barbara, All Saints Episcopal in Pasadena, Claremont School of Theology, and Inspirit Center for Spiritual Living in Orange County, among other places.

The original three-dimensional clay tablets are beautiful but also fragile and difficult to transport. To guarantee their safety and security, they are displayed in eight plexiglass vitrines. *If your church wishes to host them, let us know.* (Phone and email below.)

Two-dimensional versions of these same exquisite icons are available. With these, you and your community can pray this new practice to bring the Archetype of the Cosmic Christ alive in you. These icons are easy to transport and to post on the walls of your chapel, church, and so on. Professionally reproduced, they are available in two versions:

1. **Reproduced on semi-gloss durable paper stock**. Hang them in simple picture frames purchased on your own. Price is $495, which includes the 16 Stations on 8"x10" semi-gloss paper, plus a copy of the book, plus a video of Matthew Fox leading the practice. Add $25 for S&H. Total $520.

2. **Reproduced on aluminum.** Durable, lightweight, washable, and easy to post using 3-M removable tape. Price is $990, which includes the 16 Stations on 8"x10" molded aluminum, plus a copy of the book, plus a video of Matthew Fox leading the practice. Add $35 for S&H. Total $1,025.

Make payments to the Matthew Fox Legacy Project Inc, PO Box 424533, San Francisco, CA 94142. Or call and share your credit card information at 510-835-0655 or email *33dennis@sbcglobal.net*.

Make payments to the Matthew Fox Legacy Project Inc, PO Box 424533, San Francisco, CA 94142. Or call and share your credit card information at 510-835-0655 or email *33dennis@sbcglobal.net*.